The Kingdom of Saudi Arabia, Second Edition

UNIVERSITY PRESS OF FLORIDA

Florida A&M University, Tallahassee
Florida Atlantic University, Boca Raton
Florida Gulf Coast University, Ft. Myers
Florida International University, Miami
Florida State University, Tallahassee
New College of Florida, Sarasota
University of Central Florida, Orlando
University of Florida, Gainesville
University of North Florida, Jacksonville
University of South Florida, Tampa
University of West Florida, Pensacola

THE KINGDOM OF
SAUDI ARABIA
SECOND EDITION

David E. Long and Sebastian Maisel

UNIVERSITY PRESS OF FLORIDA

Gainesville · Tallahassee · Tampa · Boca Raton
Pensacola · Orlando · Miami · Jacksonville · Ft. Myers · Sarasota

15   14   13   12   11   10   6   5   4   3   2   1

Library of Congress Cataloging-in-Publication Data
Long, David E.
The kingdom of Saudi Arabia / David E. Long and Sebastian Maisel.—
2nd ed.
p. cm.
Includes bibliographical references and index.
ISBN 978-0-8130-3511-6 (acid-free paper)
1. Saudi Arabia. I. Maisel, Sebastian, 1970– II. Title.
DS204.L65   2010
953.8059–dc22   2010020661

The University Press of Florida is the scholarly publishing agency for the
State University System of Florida, comprising Florida A&M Univer-
sity, Florida Atlantic University, Florida Gulf Coast University, Florida
International University, Florida State University, New College of Florida,
University of Central Florida, University of Florida, University of North
Florida, University of South Florida, and University of West Florida.

University Press of Florida
15 Northwest 15th Street
Gainesville, FL 32611–2079
http://www.upf.com

To Barbara and Shannon

Contents

Illustrations

TABLES

Preface

Recorded history has witnessed scores of cataclysmic events and technological breakthroughs that have radically changed the course of human events for better and for worse. Despite the many radical changes that have occurred throughout the world, human behavioral norms have generally changed very slowly. Thus the clash between tradition and modernization is as old as the history of mankind.

During the past century, the world has witnessed more rapid social, economic, and political change than at any previous time. The Kingdom of Saudi Arabia in particular has experienced the clash between tradition and modernization to a greater degree than virtually any other country. Until the turn of the twentieth century, the political heartland of Saudi Arabia, central Arabia (called Najd), had one of the most isolated societies on earth. Najd never experienced European colonialism. The Hijaz, where Makkah (Mecca) and al-Madinah (Medina) are located, was the cradle of Islam, and although it had been host to Makkah pilgrims from all over the Muslim world, its Islamic cultural norms had not changed markedly since the time of the prophet Muhammad.

Sustained rapid change can be traumatic and threatening. The fact that Saudi Arabia has managed to maintain the delicate balance between its highly conservative Islamic values and cultural norms and its recent rapid modernization and the secularization that has inevitably followed in its wake is remarkable. Moreover, the task has become infinitely more difficult with the advent of the information technology revolution by which Saudis hear the constant harping from western commentators that "reform" in the kingdom is not moving fast enough.

All in all, the country has thus far maintained a pace that has not been too unbearably rapid for those clinging to traditional norms and not too unbearably slow for those impatient for reform. Thus the key word to characterize Saudi social, economic, and political change throughout this book is *evolution*.

The pace and direction of evolution, however, have been different in each of those categories and for each of the successive generations who have experienced it since the beginning of the oil age. The individual mix of social, economic, and political expectations has also been different for virtually every person and every age group. Another theme of the book, therefore, is that the degree of change that has evolved has not been based on current social, economic, or political conditions per se. Rather, it has been based on the degree to which expectations have been met by those conditions. The acquisition of great wealth has created expectations that cannot be sustained. For example, elder persons who grew up having to walk everywhere might be totally satisfied buying a used family car, whereas their grandson might be feel deprived because he was driving a brand-new Lexus when his best friend was driving a Ferrari. The challenge facing the country is to create more realistic public expectations that can be sustainable over time.

One should also note that evolution is a major theme in the discussion of foreign relations. For millennia, Arabian foreign relations have followed a pattern of tribal and extended family cooperation with outside groups that shared mutual interests—whether political, economic, or security matters—in seeking alliances against stronger common adversaries. As a major oil-producing country, Saudi Arabia's foreign policy interests have expanded within living memory to encompass the world. But calibrating mutual interests and antagonisms still follows much the same pattern: costing out how to balance responses to competing and often incompatible interests and animosities at the personal, family, national, and international levels. The irony is that this cost/benefit policy-making process, which they have been engaged in for millennia, is similar to what the rest of the world has been engaged in.

Finally, we should be remiss if we did not express our appreciation for all help, encouragement, enlightenment, critiques, and understanding. The list goes back over 40 years to when David first arrived in Jiddah as a junior diplomat, and it continues to the present. To avoid inadvertently leaving someone out, we wish to thank you all collectively. There are a few, however, whom we would like to acknowledge. They include Rima Hassan, at the Saudi Arabian embassy in Washington, D.C., who has continued to provide photographs for this and past publications, Frank

Verrastro, director of the Energy and National Security Program at the Center for Strategic and International Studies, and Professor Eckehard Schulz of Leipzig University, who opened the doors to Saudi Arabia for Sebastian Maisel. Another special thanks goes to Amy Gorelick of the University Press of Florida for sticking with us throughout the publication process. Most particularly, however, we wish to recognize the invaluable roles of our long-suffering wives, Barbara and Shannon, without whose support this edition likely never would have come to fruition.

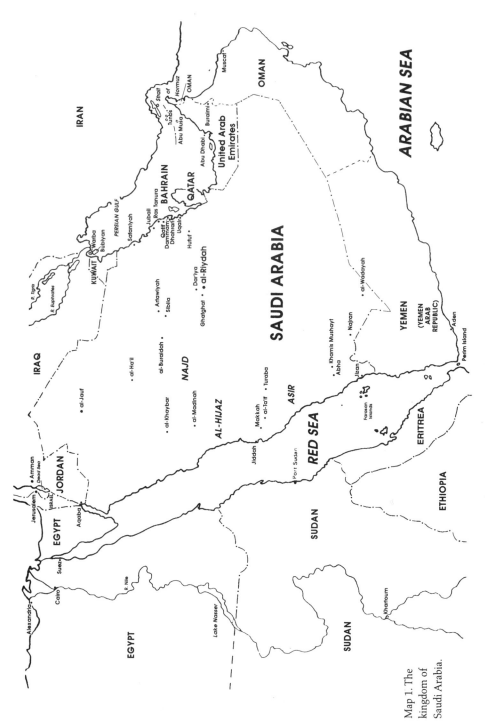

Map 1. The kingdom of Saudi Arabia.

1

The Land and People

The Kingdom of Saudi Arabia is a country of startling contrasts—a huge landmass and a small population; a barren desert terrain situated over great oil wealth; a traditional Islamic society undergoing rapid modernization; a closed society that is often in the news. Although these contrasts have evoked a good deal of fascination with the country, they have also helped to create misleading stereotypes and exacerbate the problem of understanding the country and its people.

The Saudis themselves have not made the problem any easier. Products of a closed society, they tend to keep outsiders at arm's length, and it is difficult to develop personal relationships beyond a superficial social or professional level. People who have dealt with Saudis for years can be as surprised as the casual observer by their reactions to events. Nonetheless, by seeking to look behind the stereotypes, one can glimpse the Saudis as they really are—a deeply religious, traditionally conservative, proud people who have been forced to make the transition from the preindustrial to the modern age in less than two generations.

The image of what Saudi Arabia is really like is often in the eye of the beholder. For example, most of the world is overwhelmingly interested in Saudi oil. Under the country's arid surface lie roughly 260 billion barrels of oil. That is almost one-quarter of the world's proved oil reserves, and most of it is available for export. Although it is not an overstatement to say that the developed world cannot maintain its current standard of living without Saudi oil, it is a gross overstatement to say that Saudi social values and political expectations are inextricably based on oil production. Saudi society is thoroughly Islamic and oriented to the extended family; bloodlines are ultimately more important than oil wealth.

Saudi Arabia is also an Arab state and has thus been drawn into Arab world politics, including the Arab-Israeli dispute. In this context, the kingdom has been willing to initiate punitive measures, such as the 1973–74 Arab oil embargo, when it believes they have been appropriate. However, it prefers quiet diplomacy in the search for peace.

Both quiet diplomacy and punitive measures have earned the kingdom criticism from abroad. Militant Arabs have criticized the kingdom for not adopting more confrontational policies against Israel, while Israelis and their supporters not only have condemned it for the oil embargo but have sought to link the Saudi government with militant Islamist terrorism as well, owing to a perceived relationship with al-Qaida and Osama bin Laden. They failed, however, to recognize that the Saudi government itself was a primary target of al-Qaida.

With so much attention given to oil, terrorism, and Middle East politics, few in the western world ever focused on the fact that in the Muslim world (one-fifth of the world's population) the kingdom is more important as the location of the two holiest places in Islam—Makkah (Mecca) and al-Madinah (Medina).[1] Performing the annual Hajj, or Great Pilgrimage to Makkah, is an obligation for all able Muslims once in their lives. Attended each year by 2.5 to 3 million pilgrims, the Hajj is not only one of the world's greatest religious celebrations but also one of the greatest exercises in public administration. The Saudi government is responsible for ensuring that all those who attend do so without serious injury and with a minimum of discomfort. Thus for roughly two months a year the Hajj requires virtually all the resources of the Saudi government plus those of the private sector in the Hijaz region, where it takes place.

In short, despite the internal contradictions that make generalizing so difficult, the key to understanding the kingdom is to view it on its own terms, not on the basis of why it is important to the outside world. The place to start is to examine the physical environment which has shaped the attitudes and values of Saudi society, and then look at the demographics of the people themselves.

THE LAND

Physically, Saudi Arabia occupies about 2.25 million square kilometers (865,000 square miles), making it almost one-third the size of the continental United States. Because some of its boundaries are still undefined, the exact size cannot be precisely determined. The borders with Yemen and Oman are not yet fully demarcated, although the kingdom has agreed in principle to borders with Oman and negotiated the border with Yemen.

The borders with Jordan, Iraq, and Kuwait, however, are demarcated. The Saudi-Kuwaiti neutral zone and a Saudi-Iraqi neutral zone, created in 1922 to avoid tribal border hostilities, were abolished in 1966 and 1975, respectively, and their territories were divided among the parties. A decades-old Buraymi oasis territorial dispute involving Saudi Arabia, Oman, and Abu Dhabi was settled in 1974 when Saudi Arabia agreed to give up its claim to the oasis and adjacent territory in exchange for an outlet to the Persian Gulf through Abu Dhabi.

Occupying about 80 percent of the Arabian Peninsula, Saudi Arabia abuts the Red Sea in the southwest and the Gulf in the northeast. It is bounded by Jordan to the northwest; Iraq and Kuwait to the north; Bahrain (offshore), Qatar, the United Arab Emirates, and Oman to the east; and Yemen to the south. Traditionally, land borders were relatively meaningless to Saudi rulers, who looked on sovereignty more in terms of tribal allegiance. Tribal areas were huge and only vaguely demarcated because the tribes themselves followed the rains from waterhole to waterhole and wandered over broad areas. In the 1920s, the British, as the mandatory power of Transjordan and Iraq and protecting power of Kuwait, pressured the Saudi government to accept land borders with all three countries. Later, when oil became so important in the region, the borders acquired much more importance. A deviation of a few centimeters from a common point could translate into hundreds of square kilometers when projected for long distances over the desert. Thus the discovery of oil in disputed areas has made negotiation of the remaining undemarcated borders all the more difficult.

The same can be said for offshore territorial limits. Saudi Arabia claims a 12-nautical-mile limit offshore as well as a number of islands in the Gulf and the Red Sea. With extensive oil discoveries in the Gulf, it became imperative to establish a median line between Saudi Arabia and Iran. Not until the 1970s was the line finally negotiated, however, following a number of provocative incidents involving Arabian American Oil Company (Aramco) offshore oil rigs and the Iranian navy.

Early European geographers delineated the Arabian Peninsula into two parts. Arabia Felix, or Fertile Arabia, had as its locus the relatively well-watered highlands of Yemen in the south and the adjoining mountains of Asir and the Hijaz. The rest of the peninsula was called Arabia

Deserta, or Desert Arabia. Thus, except for the western highlands, most of Saudi Arabia is desert interspersed with oases, some lying along the banks of wadis (intermittent-stream riverbeds) and others covering huge areas such as al-Hasa in the east.

With a predominantly desert terrain, a shortage of water is one of Saudi Arabia's main resource problems. In the interior are nonrenewable aquifers that are being tapped at an unprecedented rate, particularly as urbanization and population expand and agricultural development projects are created. To augment water supplies, the kingdom has created a massive water desalination system.

Despite its arid climate, sporadic rains do fall in Saudi Arabia and occasional snow in the mountains. This water has to run off somewhere; and as a result, there are numerous drainage systems made up of intersecting wadis. After local and occasionally heavy rains, the wadis can become rushing torrents. In the 1960s, a European construction company building a road in central Arabia did not construct adequate bridges. When the rains came, huge stretches of the road were washed out and the company's main field camp was flooded. By contrast, the builders of the now-defunct Hijaz railroad, which took pilgrims south from Damascus to al-Madinah before World War I, suffered no such lack of foresight. One can still see sturdy stone bridges along the abandoned rail bed spanning open desert. Among the major wadi drainage systems in the kingdom are Wadi Sirhan, located on the Saudi-Jordanian frontier; Wadi al-Batin, which flows northeast toward Kuwait; Wadi Rimah, which flows eastward from the northern Hijaz Mountains; and Wadi Dawasir and Wadi Bishah, which flow eastward from the southern Asir Mountains.

While nearly all of Saudi Arabia is arid, only part of it consists of real sand desert. There are three such deserts in the kingdom. The Nafud, sometimes called the Great Nafud, is located in the north (*nafud* is one of several Arabic words meaning "desert"); the Rub' al-Khali, literally the Empty Quarter, stretches along the entire southern frontier; and the Dahna, a long, narrow area, curves in a great arc from the Nafud westward and then south until it joins the Rub' al-Khali. The sand in all three deserts contains iron oxide, giving it a pink color that can turn to deep red in the setting sun.

The Rub' al-Khali, covering more than 550,000 square kilometers, is the largest quartz sand desert in the world. (The few local tribes call the area *al-rumal*, "the sands.") It is also one of the most forbidding and was virtually unexplored until the 1960s, when Aramco teams began searching for oil in the region.[2] Much of the Rub' al-Khali is hard-packed sand and salt flats, from which sand mountains rise as high as 300 meters. In places, these giant dunes form long, parallel ridges that extend for up to 40 kilometers (25 miles). Most of the area is uninhabited, and the Arabic dialects of those few people who live there are barely intelligible to Arabs living outside the area.

The Nafud, about 55,000 square kilometers, is made up of slightly smaller sand ridges (reaching about 90 meters in elevation) divided by flats that can extend up to 15 kilometers in width. Winter rains, when and where they happen to fall, can make these valleys lush grazing areas in the spring.

Geographically, the kingdom can be divided into five areas: central Saudi Arabia or Najd, which includes the provinces (amirates in Arabic, and provincial governors have the title *amir*) of Riyadh, Qasim and Ha'il; northwestern Arabia or the Hijaz, which includes the provinces of Makkah, al-Madinah, and Tabuk; southwestern Saudi Arabia, which includes the provinces of Asir, Baha, Jizan, and Najran; eastern Saudi Arabia, which comprises the Eastern Province (al-Mintaqah al-Sharqiyya); and northern Saudi Arabia, which includes the Northern Frontiers province (al-Huddud al-Shamaliyya) and al-Jawf. As can be seen from the geology (see below), Saudi oil reserves are found almost entirely in the Eastern Province and offshore in the Gulf.

Central Saudi Arabia: Najd

Central Arabia, or Najd, is both the geographical and the political heartland of the country. It was here that Muhammad bin Saud, amir of a tiny oasis principality, Dir'iyya, joined the Islamic revival movement of Muhammad bin Abd al-Wahhab, subsequently called Wahhabism, and laid the groundwork for the creation of the Saudi state. Najd extends westward to the Hijaz Mountains, south to the Rub' al-Khali, north to the Nafud, and east to the Dahna. Running through the center for about 600 kilometers and roughly parallel to the Dahna is Jabal Tuwaiq, a westward-facing escarpment rising 100–250 meters.

Najd, which means "highlands" in Arabic, consists mainly of sedimentary plateaus interspersed with sand deserts and low, isolated mountain ranges. The most prominent range is Jabal Shammar in the north. Until the 1920s, the Shammar tribes were under the leadership of the Al

Figure 1.1. Modern Riyadh skyline. Courtesy of Sebastian Maisel.

Figure 1.2. Old mud brick buildings in Riyadh. Used by permission of the Saudi Information Office, Washington, D.C.

Rashids of Ha'il, political rivals of the Al Saud during the late nineteenth and early twentieth centuries.

Many cities and towns are scattered throughout Najd—the largest, of course, being the national capital, al-Riyadh, on the Wadi Hanifa. Riyadh is the plural of *rawdha*, Arabic for "garden," and was so named for the number of vegetable gardens and date groves located there. From a small oasis town of about 7,500 at the turn of the century, it has grown into a major metropolis with a population approaching 4.5 million today.

Riyadh has changed incredibly in the last 40 years. In January 1967, an American engineer returned to the city after having last seen it in 1948, when it was still essentially a mud-brick city. The engineer could not recognize anything until he got to the central square in the middle of town. The city had grown by then to 200,000 people, and many of the old mud-brick houses had been torn down and replaced by drab concrete structures built by Egyptian and other Middle Eastern contractors.

Riyadh in the 1960s was still virtually closed to westerners, who numbered only about 300. In King Abd al-Aziz's lifetime, diplomats making the long trek to Riyadh for a royal audience were required to wear local Arab dress when calling at his traditional mud-brick place, the Murabba Palace. With the oil boom of the 1970s, however, the city was opened up, and by 1975, the western population numbered more than 100,000. Since then, the changes in the physical appearance of the capital have been even more startling. New buildings are constructed as fast as old ones can be torn down, and what was formerly open desert has become suburbs and shopping centers. The pace of growth has been so rapid that the ruins of Dir'iyya, the ancestral home of the Al Saud some 18 kilometers north of Riyadh, are now a virtual suburb.

Development is not limited to Riyadh. To the northeast, between Riyadh and Ha'il, is the district of Qasim, with its neighboring and rival cities of Unaizah and Buraidah. The people of Qasim are among the most conservative in the kingdom. At the same time, modernization projects have changed the face of these and other provincial towns as much as they have Riyadh. Moreover, Qasim has become the breadbasket of Saudi Arabia because of heavy public and private investment in modern, large-scale irrigated farming. The main concern regarding investment in large-scale agriculture is environmental: water resources are currently supplied by nonreplenishable aquifers.

Northwestern Saudi Arabia: The Hijaz

Saudi Arabia is bounded on the west by the Red Sea from northern Hijaz on the Gulf of Aqaba southeast to the Gulf of Aden on the Yemen coast and beyond the Arabian Sea. The entire Red Sea littoral from the Hijaz to Yemen can be divided into two topographical areas—a flat, arid yet humid coastal plain and an escarpment chain of mountains. The coastal plain, called Tihama, narrows considerably northwest of Yanbu, and in the far northwest the escarpment chain extends almost to the sea. The western face of the mountains drops off precipitously as one goes south, and the few roads climbing it wind their way past remnants of even steeper camel trails that used to be the only way to the top.

In the Hijaz, which extends roughly halfway down the Red Sea coast, the escarpment highlands are called the Hijaz Mountains. They do not exceed 2,000 meters (6,400 feet) and are generally much lower as one travels north. The eastern side of the mountains falls off gradually toward the Najdi plateau. Also on the eastern side of the Hijaz Mountains are a number of huge lava fields (*harrat*) where the terrain looks like a lunar landscape. The largest, Harrat Khaybar, is just north of al-Madinah.

The Hijaz (*hijaz* means "barrier" or "boundary" in Arabic) was an independent state until it was conquered by King Abd al-Aziz in 1924 and annexed in 1926. Then as now, its life revolved around Islam. Within the region are located the two holiest cities in Islam, Makkah and al-Madinah. One of the five basic pillars (tenets) of Islam is the Hajj, or Great Pilgrimage to Makkah, and over the centuries a pilgrim service industry evolved that was the backbone of the pre-Saudi Hijazi economy and before oil of the Saudi monarchy as well.

Makkah and al-Madinah are forbidden to non-Muslims. With the presence of Muslims from all over the world, however, they possess a cosmopolitan atmosphere that could rival any major city in the world. The Saudi government has spent billions upgrading the holy sites in both cities to accommodate the ever-increasing millions of pilgrims who visit the holy cities each year.

Jiddah on the Red Sea coast has been the traditional port of entry for the Hajj. The name is Arabic for "grandmother," and according to tradition, Eve was buried there. The tomb of Eve was visited by many pilgrims during the Hajj until King Abd al-Aziz had it demolished as heretical.

Figure 1.3. Modern Jiddah skyline. Used by permission of the Saudi Information Office, Washington, D.C.

Before the oil era, it was a small city noted for its multistoried Turkish-style houses decorated with wood carvings and latticework.

Long a financial and commercial hub due to the Hajj, Jiddah was the largest city in the kingdom before Riyadh was opened up to expatriates in the 1970s. Although Riyadh has eclipsed it as the kingdom's financial and diplomatic center, Jiddah is still a major seaport, a commercial hub, and the principal port of entry for the Hajj and for the Hijaz in general. Moreover, its mercantile mentality is readily apparent. By 2009 its estimated population exceeded 3.5 million, and it was replete with skyscrapers, urban renewal, and city beautification.

The major city in the mountains is Ta'if, just east of Makkah. Because of its balmy winter climate, Ta'if has become an informal "summer capital" for those wishing to get out of Riyadh or Jiddah but not leave the country.

Under the Saudis, the Hijaz has been divided into three provinces: Makkah Province in the south, al-Madinah Province in the center, and Tabuk Province in the north. Jeddah is the major seaport for all three provinces. However, Yanbu, which has been the traditional port for al-

Figure 1.4. King Fahd Fountain, Jiddah. Courtesy of David Long.

Figure 1.5. Old Jiddah. Used by permission of the Saudi Information Office, Washington, D.C.

Madinah, has increased in size and importance as the terminus of an oil pipeline from the Eastern Province to the Red Sea. In recent years, construction has begun on a modern city and a technical school near the town of Rabigh, north of Jiddah.

Eastern Saudi Arabia: The Eastern Province

Historically, the most important populated area in the east was al-Hasa oasis. Al-Hasa (or its variant, al-Ahsa) means "sandy ground with water close to the surface."[3] The term aptly describes the area between the Dahna and the Gulf coast and extending to the Rub' al-Khali, the area now designated by the Saudis as the Eastern Province.

Immediately east of the Dahna is the Summan plateau, a barren, wind-blown area of ancient watercourses and occasional mountains. East of the plateau is a broad, flat, gravelly coastal plain that extends to an irregular coastline marked by numerous *sabkhas*, or salt flats. Sand hills are dispersed throughout the plain, expanding into the Jafura, a small sand desert that joins the Rub' al-Khali in the south.

Al-Hasa oasis, located inland from the coast, is the largest oasis in the world, and its major town, Hufuf, is both an agricultural center and a residence for oil field workers. A smaller oasis, Qatif (and its principal town of the same name), is located to the north on the Gulf coast. The two oases are home to most of Saudi Arabia's Shi'ites, many of whom, particularly from Qatif, have found employment with Aramco since the earliest days of the company.

The primary significance of the region is that underneath it lies the bulk of Saudi Arabia's huge oil reserves. The Ghawar field, which stretches for more than 200 kilometers from north to south, is the largest single oil field in the world. The economy of the Eastern Province is predominantly based on oil, and even recent efforts to diversify the industrial base focus on petrochemical industries.

Far to the south in the Rub' al-Khali is the Shaybah oil field, which came on stream in 1998 and is piped 638 kilometers to Abqaiq, a major Saudi Aramco oil installation inland from the Gulf. The main camp at Shaybah, which includes administration offices, facilities for about 1,000 employees, workshops, and an airstrip, is surrounded by huge pink sand dunes rising over 250 meters. Yet at their base is a prehistoric salt flat in the middle of the desert where saltwater can be welled to be pumped back into the field to maintain pressure. The oil itself is "extra light,"

Figure 1.6. Corniche Drive, Dammam, Eastern Province. Used by permission of the Saudi Information Office, Washington, D.C.

which according to one Saudi Aramco worker, "you could almost put it in the tank of your truck and drive away it is such high grade."[4]

The capital and principal city of the province is Dammam, just south of Qatif. Once a small pearling and privateering port, it is now a bustling metropolis. South of Dammam is Dhahran, whose name is far more familiar in the West. It is actually not a city but the location of Saudi Aramco headquarters, King Faysal University, the American Consulate General, and Dhahran International Airport. Nearby, on the coast, is al-Khobar, which grew from virtually nothing to an important industrial service city.

Located along the coast north of Dammam to the Kuwaiti border are a number of oil facilities, beginning with Ras Tanura, the principal Saudi Aramco oil terminal, and extending to Khafji in what was once part of the Saudi-Kuwaiti Neutral Zone until it was abolished in 1966. Just north of Ras Tanura is Jubail, the site of the first disembarkation of American oilmen, who waded ashore in 1933 to what was then a small village. Today it is the site of much of Saudi Arabia's petrochemical industry and the Saudi navy's principal Gulf naval base, all constructed within the last 20 years. South of Dhahran is the small town of Uqair. Largely overlooked by recent development, it was at one time, with Qatif and Jubail, a principal port for trade with Najd and the site of several early political meetings between King Abd al-Aziz and the British.

Southwestern Saudi Arabia

The topography of southwestern Saudi Arabia is an extension of the rest of the Arabian coast of the Red Sea and inland mountain chain. But as the mountains increase in elevation, the region resembles Yemen more than the rest of the kingdom. The highest point in the kingdom is Jabal Sawda (Black Mountain), which exceeds 3,000 meters. The kingdom has built a national park along its crest.

Throughout the mountains there are trees and flowing streams and distinctive fortresslike adobe brick houses inlayed with layers of stone to protect against the monsoon rains from the south and decorated with

Figure 1.7. Traditional stone and mud brick house, Asir. Note the flat perpendicular stones arranged to keep rainwater off the mud brick. Courtesy of David Long.

Figure 1.8. Cable car, Asir Mountains. Courtesy of David Long.

whitewashed turrets and window and door frames. Green terraced fields cling to steep mountainsides where crops and fruit trees are grown. Further south, the eastern face of the mountains falls away to the Rub' al-Khali.

As noted, this region consists of four Saudi provinces. The largest is province Asir, annexed by King Abd al-Aziz in 1930. Its capital, Abha, just southeast of Jabal Sawda, was the hub of the pre-Saudi principality of Asir and is still the largest city in the region. Not far from Abha is Khamis Mushayt, site of a major Saudi military cantonment.

The former Saudi provincial amir, Khalid Al Faysal (now amir of Makkah), developed a tourist industry. Abha and the surrounding mountains have become a regional summer resort where families in Arabia can enjoy the balmy summer climate and the husbands can easily commute back home if business requires. There are excellent hotels and even a hotel management institute in Abha that also has an artists' colony.

North of Asir is Baha, the smallest of all Saudi provinces. It extends from the mountains down to Tihama. Like Asir, it has a mild summer climate with forests and streams in the mountains. Its proximity to the Hijaz makes it also a tourist center for Saudis and other Gulf states. Most of the people native to the area are members of two tribal confederations, the Ghamid and the Zahran.

The two remaining provinces in the region are Najran and Jizan. Najran is located in the southeast on the Yemen border. Most of the arable land lies in a broad valley through which flows a seasonal river that rises in the Yemen highlands. Its waters are used for irrigation, and the Saudi government has built a dam across it to conserve the water supply, much of which formerly disappeared into the Rub' al-Khali. The province of Jizan is located in the Tihama far below Abha. It is named after its capital, which has long been the major seaport for Asir.

Figure 1.9. Qasr al-Amarah, former governor's palace, Najran. Courtesy of David Long.

Figure 1.10. Dumat al-Jandal with the early Mosque of Omar in the foreground, Jauf Province. Courtesy of David Long.

In 1933, King Abd al-Aziz annexed Najran and Asir, which resulted in a brief war with Yemen in 1934. In the Treaty of Ta'if of 1934, Yemen agreed to Saudi sovereignty over Asir and Najran, but border disputes continued. However, border tensions have eased since a memorandum of understanding on borders was signed by both countries in 2000.

Northern Saudi Arabia

In the area extending along the kingdom's northern borders are two Saudi provinces, al-Jawf and Northern Frontiers (al-Huddud al-Shamaliyya). In ancient times, the main east-west caravan route from the Mediterranean and Arabia to the Orient passed through the region, used by the Nabataeans among others. In 762, however, the route moved north through Baghdad when the Abbasid Caliphate declared it their new capital, and what is now northern Saudi Arabia became somewhat of a backwater.

It is physically isolated from the rest of the country by the Nafud. Topographically a part of the Syrian Desert, the area's tribes claim kinship with fellow tribes in neighboring Jordan, Iraq, and Syria, occasionally owning passports from all three countries. In the northernmost part of the country, the Wadi Sirhan forms a great depression, extending northward into Jordan.

There are two major towns in al-Jawf: the provincial capital, Sakaka, and Dumat al-Jandal, where there is an ancient fortress, Qasr al-Marid, and one of the oldest mosques in Saudi Arabia, Masjid al-Omar, thought to be a Christian church in pre-Islamic times. Near Sakaka are Neolithic stone megaliths at a desert site, al-Rajajil, evidence of how long the area has been inhabited. The capital of the Northern Frontiers is Ar'ar, once a settlement for King Abd al-Aziz's Ikhwan tribal forces.

Before the 1967 Arab-Israeli war, the most important installation in the region economically was the Trans-Arabian Pipeline (Tapline), which carried crude oil from the Eastern Province to the Lebanese port of Sidon. With that route closed due to Israeli occupation in southern Syria (the Golan Heights), Tapline has lost much of its economic importance, although oil is still sent through the pipeline to Jordan.

CLIMATE

Saudi Arabia has the harsh, hot climate that one associates with a desert area. There are variations, however. In the interior, the lack of humidity causes daytime temperatures to rise sharply, and readings can register more than 54 degrees C (130 degrees F). The same lack of humidity also causes temperatures to drop precipitously after the sun goes down, sometimes as much as 20 degrees C (70 degrees F) in less than three hours. Subfreezing temperatures are common in winter, and the ever-present winds create a wind chill that can be very cold for those not properly dressed.

The coastal areas combine heat and high humidity. The humidity usually keeps the temperature from exceeding about 40 degrees C in the summer but likewise prevents it from dropping more than a few degrees at night. Thus summer days and nights are steamy and unpleasant. Winter temperatures, on the other hand, are warmer and balmier at night than they are in the interior, particularly along the Red Sea. Along the coasts and in the interior, rainfall is sporadic. Torrential rains can flood one area while entirely missing areas a few kilometers away. At other times, the same area can go without rain for 5–10 years. The sporadic nature of the rains is why desert pastoralists must cover wide areas in search of pasture for their livestock.

The mountain areas are cooler, particularly in Asir, where it can get quite cold at night. The Asir also gets the moisture-laden monsoon winds from the south in the winter, when most of its annual rain falls (about 500 millimeters).

GEOLOGY

Because of Saudi Arabia's vast oil reserves, mention should be made about its geology. The Arabian Peninsula consists of a single tectonic plate, the Arabian plate, which has been slowly moving eastward. The mountain ranges that parallel the Red Sea coastal plain are among the oldest geological strata there is, called the pre-Cambrian shield, which is located just above the earth's core. These mountains are one of the few places on earth where this stratum appears above ground, and thus there is no way that oil deposits could be found there. But as the Arabian plate shifted to the east, it thrust under what was a large ancient sea, pushing onward over millions of years until all that was left of it was the Gulf. As the ancient seabed was pushed thousands of meters under the earth's surface, the sedimentary deposits of plant and sea life materials that drifted to the sea's floor came under enormous pressure. And that process is what created the oil reserves throughout the entire Gulf littoral.

THE PEOPLE

Official Saudi census figures placed the population at 16.9 million in December 1992, of which 12.3 million were Saudis and 4.6 million foreigners. This number had increased to 22.7 million by 2004, of which 16.5 million were Saudis. Although the population is relatively small in comparison with the country's great wealth, official Saudi estimates show that it is growing at about 3.7 percent a year, one of the highest rates in the world. Unless it begins to level out, the kingdom may face a major socioeconomic problem in the next century as more and younger Saudis chase fewer and fewer jobs. Increasing numbers of unemployed or underemployed young people—while their basic needs are being met by their families—are beginning to feel marginalized, frustrated, and resentful of the establishment, not for what it does but because they are not a part of it. It is such people who become willing listeners to the militant political message of the radical Islamists.

The indigenous Saudi population is among the most homogeneous in the Middle East. Virtually all Saudis are Arab and Muslim. Of course, this fact is not surprising when one considers that the Arabian Peninsula is the cradle of both Arabism and Islam. The only non-Muslims are expatriates who are in the country either doing business on contract or representing home governments; they are not permanent residents. Bloodlines, not geography, determine nationality, and being born in Saudi Arabia does not automatically entitle a person to citizenship.

The importance of bloodlines is a manifestation of the basically tribal nature of Saudi society. Tribal in this context refers to genealogy, not to occupation or politics. The days when the tribes were an independent political force have long gone, their power forever broken by King Abd al-Aziz. Even before modern urbanization, Saudi political power emanated mainly from sturdy yeomen villagers in Najd, not from nomads. But the villagers also had tribal affiliations.

The extended family rather than the clan or tribe is the most important social institution in Saudi Arabia. If put to the test, loyalty to one's extended family would probably even exceed loyalty to the state. After all, the state has been in existence for a few decades, and most Saudis trace their families back for centuries. Extended families often live together in the major cities in large family compounds. With the high cost of real estate, however, and as each succeeding generation brings more nuclear families, that practice is becoming increasingly difficult to maintain.

Saudi family dynamics are still overwhelmingly traditional and contrast sharply with practices based on contemporary western social values. This is particularly so in gender relations. Much has been written in the western popular press about the inferior role of women in Saudi society, and indeed many younger women find many traditional social practices oppressive. These practices should be viewed from their proper perspective, however, and not simply from that of western values. In the traditional Islamic Saudi family, men control business and public affairs while women control the home. (Women can own their own property, however, and manage it as they wish.)

There are few areas of the world where women are as domineering in the home as Saudi women are. On family decisions, they tend to present a solid front that men dare not ignore with impunity. There is generally a matriarch—a grandmother or mother-in-law—who rules the home, and not even her sons care to thwart her wishes. For example, the mother of King Fahd expected and received daily visits from her sons when they were in town, no matter how busy their schedules. And it is the matriarch rather than the husband who imposes the most onerous restrictions on a young wife.

The trade-off for women's power inside the home is virtually no mobility to pursue outside interests. There is almost no contact between the sexes in public, where women must be veiled and are not even allowed to drive automobiles. Job opportunities for women are scarce and restricted to a few areas where they deal only with other women. Given the prevalence of traditional social values in the kingdom at present, most Saudi women would probably not be willing to sacrifice their control inside the home for greater mobility. But how long this attitude will predominate is an open question, particularly with over half of the population under age 15 and a growing number of women receiving higher education. Moreover, young men are increasingly supportive of more mobility for women, if for no other reason than economics. For example, with rapid population growth and declining economic opportunities, the expense of hiring a driver to take the women out while the men are at work is becoming a growing burden for younger families. There appears to be no desire, even among the most modernized Saudi women, to abandon traditional Islamic social values. But within the traditional social framework, significant change in what is considered acceptable behavior for women seems only a matter of time.

With genealogy so important, there is relatively little social mobility in Saudi Arabia. Najd is the center of Saudi political power, and its tribal affiliations are among the most aristocratic on the Arabian Peninsula. Members of the leading tribal families of Najd are at the top of the social order, and nontribal families and descendants of former slaves are near the bottom. This does not mean that members of the latter classes cannot rise to positions of power. The finance minister under King Saud, Muhammad Surrur Sabban, came from a former slave family, yet he became one of the wealthiest and most influential men in the kingdom.

Historically, slavery in Arabia, although certainly a violation of human rights, was never the inhumane institution that it was in the West. Even though their masters owned them, slaves still had more status, derived from their owners, than nontribal people did, and their owners had the responsibility of caring for their welfare. When Prince Faysal, then acting as prime minister, formally abolished slavery in 1962, many slaves, particularly of the royal family, refused to go. When asked years later if he had served the king, one man asserted, "I am no servant. I am a slave!"[5]

The population of the Hijaz is far more cosmopolitan than Najd, due to centuries of immigration connected with the Hajj. The leading families formed a merchant class that grew up in the Hijaz to serve the Hajj. Their origins were far more varied than those of Najdis, with fewer tribal affiliations, although many could trace their lineage as far back as Najdis could. The Hadhrami community is an example of nonindigenous residents in the Hijaz. Most of them came to the Hijaz from the Wadi Hadhramawt in the southern part of Yemen within the past 100 years, although some go back much further.

With the concentration of the oil industry in the Eastern Province, that area has developed a polyglot population that equals the Hijaz's. Many of the pre-oil families had close family ties to other Gulf states, particularly Bahrain. The Qusaybi (Gosaibi) family, for example, has a large branch in Bahrain as well as in the Eastern Province.

The Eastern Province is the home of the only significant minority in the kingdom, the Shi'ite community, which numbers between 500,000 and 600,000. They live mainly in al-Qatif oasis on the Gulf coast and inland in al-Hasa oasis. Unlike much of the population, Shi'ites are willing to work with their hands, and over the years they have become the backbone of the skilled and semiskilled oil industry workforce. Under Aramco, discrimination by the Sunni majority was greatly mitigated.

Uninterested in inter-Arab politics during the tumultuous 1960s, the Shi'as were considered excellent security risks for sensitive technical jobs. With the Iranian revolution in 1979, however, concern increased that they could become a fifth column for the revolutionary Shi'a politics of Iran, undermining security in the Eastern Province. Of particular concern was the younger generation, which took for granted the social and economic gains Aramco had given their fathers and grandfathers. The younger generation apparently sparked the disturbances in November 1979 and the riots in February 1980. Iranian propaganda in Arabic is beamed at the Shi'ite community from Radio Tehran and Radio Ahwaz and is a regular topic of conversation in the Husayniyas, Shi'ite religious study centers that are a major feature of Shi'ite social life as well.

To date, fears about the loyalty of the Shi'a community have not been realized. Not only did the government belatedly invest more money in infrastructure in Shi'a areas, but the Shi'a community itself proved highly suspicious of the revolutionary regime in Tehran. Thus they perceived the Iran-Iraq war as an Arab-Persian conflict more than a Sunni-Shi'ite conflict. From their perspective, they are Arabs, not Persians; and while they might be second-class Saudi citizens, they still have attained a level of prosperity that they would not wish to give up for the harsh, theocratic rule they see in Iran, even with the remote possibility that such a regime could be carved out of predominantly Sunni Saudi Arabia.

A few families of non-Arabian origin have also become Saudi nationals. Most are found in the Hijaz and are descended from Hajjis who never returned to their homelands after the pilgrimage. Some of these families have lived in Jiddah and Makkah for centuries and have attained stature in society and high rank in government, mainly associated with the Hajj.

Others, of more recent vintage, have eked out a living as unskilled laborers. At the time when Abd al-Aziz conquered the Hijaz, thousands of these people lived around Jiddah in cardboard villages. Some would stay only long enough to earn enough money to begin their return home, mainly to Africa; others were more or less permanent residents. Over time, the Saudi regime tightened its entry and resident requirements and repatriated most of these Hajji laborers.

An interesting group of non-Arabs that have become Saudi nationals are the central Asian community, often collectively called "Turkistanis," "Tashkandis," or "Bukharis" after areas and cities in former Soviet Central Asia. They are descendants of a group of political refugees who escaped overland from the Soviet Union in the 1920s. Fiercely anti-Communist and devoutly Muslim, the community took refuge in several countries before finally ending up in Saudi Arabia. Because of their faith, loyalty, and disinterest in inter-Arab politics, many of them were accepted into the Saudi military and security services.

Another group of naturalized Saudis are the descendants of a remarkable group of non-Saudi Arabs who came to Saudi Arabia for various reasons in the 1930s. These included Rashad Pharaoun, a Syrian who originally came to serve as the personal physician to King Abd al-Aziz and remained to become a senior advisor; Yusif Yassin, a Syrian who became deputy foreign minister under Prince (later King) Faysal; and Hafiz al-Wahba, an Egyptian who also became a senior advisor.

The distinction between "foreigners" and "natives" breaks down somewhat when looking at neighboring states—for example, the Hadhrami community in the Hijaz and the Eastern Province families with ties in other Gulf states. Indeed, many of the old Sunni families of Kuwait and Bahrain migrated from Najd some 300 years ago. Northern Saudis have close tribal ties in Jordan, Syria, and Iraq. All these ties are reflected during the Hajj, when members of the Gulf Cooperation Council (GCC) states are not required to obtain Hajj visas. No matter how long one's family has resided in the country, however, one is still identified by the family's original place of origin.

The expatriate community, numbering between 4 and 5 million, comprises between one-fourth and one-third of the total population. Before the oil boom of the 1970s, the Eastern Province probably had the largest concentration of expatriates because that is where the oil industry is located. At one time, Aramco employed literally thousands of expatriates.

Most of the rest of the expatriates were historically located in the Hijaz, then the economic and diplomatic center of the country. When Riyadh was opened up to development in the 1970s, it became the largest city in the kingdom and now probably contains the most expatriates.

Most expatriates in Saudi Arabia are from nearby Middle Eastern countries, South Asia, and the Philippines and are mainly skilled and unskilled laborers and service industry personnel. Despite relatively harsh living conditions, there is virtually an unending supply of menial foreign labor. Economic opportunity is still much greater than at home, and in many cases working conditions at home are equally harsh or worse. The Yemeni community was formerly the largest, estimated as high as 1 million. Its numbers were drastically reduced following Operation Desert Storm, both for security reasons and in retaliation for Yemen's political sympathies toward Saddam Hussein. At present, however, Yemeni workers are again being allowed into the kingdom.

The status of western executives and technicians is much higher. Nevertheless, isolation from a generally closed Saudi society, puritanical social norms, and the lack of physical mobility (particularly for women) make family life for westerners who are used to more permissive societies difficult despite high salaries.

There has been speculation about how many foreign workers pose a threat to the regime through the spread of liberal political and social ideas. In fact, their political and social impact on Saudi society appears to be slight. There is virtually no social contact between Saudis and skilled and semiskilled workers, and the closed nature of Saudi society makes contact with white-collar, mostly western expatriates minimal also. Moreover, foreign workers of all classes are in the kingdom primarily to make money and then return home, not to make political converts.

There are some exceptions to the lack of social interaction between Saudis and foreigners. The large numbers of public school teachers imported in past years, particularly from Syria and Egypt, have served as a conduit for spreading militant Islamic political teachings, even though Saudis are now increasingly replacing foreign teachers. Perhaps a greater potential danger to internal stability, however, is the economic frustration of a growing number of expatriates who have experienced late or deferred payments for services rendered, spurred by Saudi financial problems.

How long the traditional patterns of Saudi society will remain entrenched is an open question. Saudi society, which was at a preindustrial level just a few decades ago, is rushing into modernity at an unbelievable pace. The impact of development on the society is everywhere present. Urbanization is bringing people to the cities, where they are cut off from the support systems of traditional society. Modern communications and transportation have brought the world to the doorstep of what had long been one of the most remote and isolated countries on earth. The evolution of Riyadh into the economic as well as political hub of the country has brought Saudis from all over the kingdom and foreign workers and professionals from all over the world, making it a highly cosmopolitan city. It is not uncommon for families to have several houses scattered over the kingdom, reflecting job, government, and place of origin.

The miracle is not how much Saudi society has changed; it would be inconceivable to assume that great changes had not occurred. What is really extraordinary is how resilient the society has been in the face of change. The extended family system is still intact and indeed is probably the most stabilizing force in the country. Whatever Saudi Arabia's political or economic future, it is difficult to visualize without the paramount importance of extended family ties.

2

Historical Background

Western scholarship on Saudi Arabia is a relatively recent phenomenon. While some of it is very good, little of it adequately conveys a sense of historical tradition. Personal accounts of early western travelers to Arabia are often a better way to get a feel for the history of the country before it was cluttered up with fast-food restaurants, 747s, satellite television, and other western contributions to world culture. These early travelers included Carsten Niebuhr, who wrote detailed accounts of his travels to Arabia in the eighteenth century, Sir Richard Burton, who wrote a fascinating nineteenth-century account of sneaking into Makkah (Mecca) during the hajj; Charles Doughty, whose prose evokes the image of an Old Testament prophet; and the prolific H. St. John B. Philby, who first came to Arabia during World War I. If one reads Arabic, the great eighteenth- and nineteenth-century Najdi chroniclers such as Husayn Ibn Ghannam and Uthman Ibn Bishr are another source of historical tradition.[1] Although they lack western standards of historiography, they convey a true sense of the timelessness of culture and conflict behind the rapid, indeed breathtaking, pace of modernization during the past quarter century.

Two strains of tradition are inseparably bound to the political history of Saudi Arabia: family and religion. As noted in chapter 1, family tradition is as old as Arabia itself. Religious tradition dates to the founding of Islam in the seventh century. The two came together in the mid-eighteenth century in the persons of Muhammad bin Saud and Muhammad bin Abd al-Wahhab. Muhammad bin Saud (bin means "son of" in Arabic) was the founder of the Al Saud, or House of Saud, the royal family of Saudi Arabia. Muhammad bin Abd al-Wahhab was the founder of what is widely known as the Wahhabi revival movement. His descendants are the second most prestigious family in Saudi Arabia after the royal family and are called the Al al-Shaykh, or House of the Shaykh. (The surname comes from the fact that Muhammad bin Abd al-Wahhab was called "the Teacher" or al-Shaykh in Arabic.)[2] The fusing of temporal power represented by the Al Saud and spiritual power represented by the Al al-Shaykh has sustained Saudi political cohesion from that time to the present.

SHAYKH MUHAMMAD BIN ABD AL-WAHHAB AND HIS REVIVAL MOVEMENT

Muhammad bin Abd al-Wahhab, born in 1703/4 in Uyayna, a small oasis town on the Wadi Hanifa in Najd, was a member of the Bani Sinan tribe, which had been in central Arabia since antiquity.[3] Like his father, Abd al-Wahhab bin Sulaiman, he was a noted scholar and a follower of the then largely forgotten Hanbali school of Sunni Islamic jurisprudence.

Muhammad was something of a child prodigy, memorizing the entire Quran by the age of 10. He married at 12 and settled down early to a life of scholarship. Najd may have been physically isolated in those days, but not intellectually. Muhammad traveled, absorbing ideas from the outside Islamic world. He performed the hajj to Makkah, going on to al-Madinah (Medina), and also visited Basra, Baghdad, and Damascus. In al-Hasa oasis, he studied under Shaykh Abdullah bin Ibrahim al-Najdi, a noted scholar who later moved to al-Madinah, where he became known as al-Madani (the man from Madinah).

At the heart of the revival movement is the Islamic doctrine of *tawhid* (strict monotheism). It also condemns innovations (*bid'a*), or false practices that crept into Islam over the centuries. Ibn Abd al-Wahhab called them polytheistic in contrast to the strict monotheism of Islam. He particularly decried a common practice of the time: venerating noted holy men and making pilgrimages to their tombs, usually domed structures whose custodians profited from tourism. To this day, Saudis, including the royal family, bury their dead in unmarked graves lest the tomb of some revered family member become a holy shrine.

Although Shaykh Muhammad rejected the supremacy of any single Sunni school of Islamic jurisprudence, his reform movement was firmly based on Hanbali law, the most conservative in personal and family law of the four recognized Sunni schools. (For a discussion of Islamic law in Saudi Arabia, see chapter 3.) The movement is now generally called Wahhabism, a term first used by its detractors. To this day, many of the followers of the revival take offense at being called Wahhabis, believing that it denotes the deification of the movement's founder and is a desecration of the sovereignty of God. They prefer to be called Muwahhidin (monotheists or unitarians).

Ibn Abd al-Wahhab was greatly influenced by the writings of an early Hanbali reformer, Taqi al-Din Ahmad ibn Taymiyya (1262–1328). Ibn Taymiyya lived at a time when the centralized Abbasid caliphate of Baghdad had collapsed and many petty Muslim rulers were seeking *fatwas* from local religious authorities—often through bribes—declaring their legitimacy as independent rulers. He denounced this practice and claimed that political legitimacy came only from strict adherence to the fundamental teachings of Shari'a law. It is not surprising, therefore, that Ibn Taymiyya spent most of his adult life in jail.

Ibn Taymiyya was not just another puritan fundamentalist, however. Beginning in the ninth century, most Sunni Islamic jurists ceased to recognize independent reasoning (*ijtihad*) as an authoritative means of interpreting Islamic law. He not only rejected what was called the "closing of the door of independent reasoning" but also claimed to be a *mujtahid*, a qualified practitioner of ijtihad. Ibn Abd al-Wahhab incorporated into his reform movement Ibn Taymiyya's call for a return to the fundamentals of Islam and rejection of false innovations, as well as the use of independent reasoning in interpreting Islamic law.[4]

Ibn Abd al-Wahhab returned to his native Uyayna around 1744 and began preaching against what he believed was the lax behavior of the townspeople and their disregard for Islamic law. His preaching could be said to have been the beginning of his puritanical Islamic reform movement. However, his uncompromising Puritanism was not popular in Uyayna, and he was quickly expelled from his native town. Forced to seek another place from which to preach his revival, he soon found himself in the nearby town of Dir'iyya (now a suburb of Riyadh). He was invited to stay by the local *amir*, Muhammad bin Saud, who had become a convert. Thus began the collaboration between spiritual and temporal powers that has lasted to this day. Muhammad bin Abd al-Wahhab died in Dir'iyya in 1792.

AMIR MUHAMMAD BIN SAUD AND THE CREATION
OF THE FIRST SAUDI STATE

Genealogy is very important in Arabia. The purest bloodlines, mythological or otherwise, are considered to be those traced back to two ancient figures: Qahtan, whose descendants generally (although not inevitably) settled in southern Arabia, and Adnan, whose descendants settled in northern Arabia. The Al Saud traces its ancestry to Bakr bin Wa'il bin Rabi'a bin Nazar bin Ma'ad bin Adnan. The family reportedly moved from Qatif oasis in eastern Arabia to Najd in about 1450. The founder of the royal house, Muhammad bin Saud bin Muqrin bin Markhan, was born about 1703/4. By the time he met Muhammad bin Abd al-Wahhab in 1744, he had been for two years the amir of Dir'iyya, a petty principality just down the Wadi Hanifa from Uyayna.

The Wahhabi reform movement that he embraced quickly attracted other converts, particularly desert warriors for whom tribal warfare was a way of life and which the movement raised to a level of high moral imperative. Under the banner of tawhid, they began to convert the Najdi tribes and transform the traditional and constant condition of Bedouin warfare into a holy cause. For the rest of his reign, Amir Muhammad constantly engaged in warfare. By the time he died in 1765, most of Najd had come under his rule, including Uyayna, where Muhammad bin Abd al-Wahhab personally chose the governor to succeed Uthman, the ruler who had exiled him. Uthman was put to death by followers of the new revival movement.

So long as political expansion was limited to central Arabia, it went largely unnoticed by the outside world. But under Muhammad bin Saud's son, Abd al-Aziz (1719/20–1803), and his grandson, Saud (died 1814), Muwahhidin warriors ranged far beyond Najd, and the family domains were expanded to include most of the Arabian Peninsula. In 1801, the Muwahhidin sacked the town of Karbala, a Shi'a holy city in what is now southern Iraq. They destroyed the large domed tombs of various Shi'a holy men, including the tomb of the prophet Muhammad's grandson, Husayn, one of the most venerated of all Shi'a "saints." Indeed, Shi'as consider Karbala and the tomb of Husayn to be the third holiest site in Islam after Makkah and al-Madinah. Two years later, in 1803, the Al Sauds captured Makkah from the Hashemites, descendants of the prophet Muhammad who had ruled in Makkah for centuries and were then under the suzerainty of the Ottoman sultans. The Al Sauds were forced to withdraw from the Hijaz when plague decimated their army, but they retook it in 1806. They allowed the Hashemite ruler, Sharif Ghalib, to remain as governor.

To the east, the Muwahhidin pushed all the way to Oman, where they forced the Omani sultan to pay tribute. As the revival movement gained adherents in the Gulf, Muwahhidin privateers began sailing out with increasing zeal to prey on the merchant shipping of unbelievers. Privateering was not merely profitable; from their viewpoint, they had a religious duty to oppose evil by attacking the shipping of non-Muslim unbelievers and non-Muwahhidin Muslim "heretics"—a sort of religious bounty hunting. However, the British, who had become the principal western maritime power in the region and who were forced to defend the sea lanes to their empire in India, considered the Muwahhidin to be pirates. Thus the Gulf littoral that is now part of the United Arab Emirates earned the sobriquet "the Pirate Coast."

In a relatively short period of about 60 years, the Saudi regime had been transformed from a tiny oasis principality to an important Middle Eastern state. It is interesting to speculate on what might have happened if the Saudis had possessed the military technology to match their ideological zeal. This same mixture of courage and ideological fervor must have enabled the original armies of Islam to topple empires and expand all the way from Spain to Indonesia.

Such an event was not to happen, however. The Saudi capture of the Muslim holy places was seen as an affront by the Ottoman caliphate. It also deprived the Ottomans of considerable revenues. They asked the ruler of Egypt, Muhammad Ali, who was technically the Ottoman viceroy, to recover the Hijaz and invade Najd. Muhammad Ali harbored his own territorial ambitions in Arabia and in 1811 dispatched an army under his son, Tusun. After several years of fighting, the Egyptians finally retook the Hijaz with the holy cities of Makkah and al-Madinah, but they were not able to subjugate the Muwahhidin. Then in 1814 Amir Saud died, and his son, Abdullah bin Saud (reigned 1814–18), retreated to the Najdi heartland.

In 1816, Muhammad Ali sent a second son, Ibrahim Pasha, with a well-equipped army to invade Najd. After two years, Ibrahim entered what was left of Dir'iyya and the first Saudi state came to an end. Abdullah bin Saud was sent in exile to Cairo and later to Constantinople, where he was beheaded. Dir'iyya was totally destroyed; its palm groves were cut down and burned. It never recovered, and its ruins can still be seen about 20 kilometers north of Riyadh.

In the Gulf, Muwahhidin privateers were left to fend for themselves. In December 1818, the British, who had already attempted several times to put them down, assembled a large naval and land force at Ras al-Khaymah on the Pirate Coast that was finally able to defeat them. In 1820, the local amirs agreed to a truce banning privateering. The agreement also created the basis for British hegemony in what was called the Trucial States. British protection lasted there until 1971, when they gained independence as the United Arab Emirates.

THE RISE AND FALL OF THE SECOND SAUDI STATE

Although the destruction of Dir'iyya seemed to herald the end of the Al Saud as a political force in Najd, such was not the case. In 1824, Abdullah's great-uncle, Turki bin Abdullah (reigned 1824–34), again assembled an army of tribal warriors under the banner of tawhid and drove the Egyptian garrisons from Najd. He did not return to Dir'iyya, however, but established himself at Riyadh, which has remained the Saudi capital to this day.

The birth, fall, and rebirth of the Saudi state began a pattern that was to continue down to the reign of the present king's father, Abd al-Aziz. After a period of territorial expansion, internecine rivalries within the family would undermine the regime, and outsiders would seize power; then, after a time, a new Saudi leader would appear to repair the family fortunes and regain its patrimony. The process began again in 1834 with the assassination of Amir Turki by a member of a collateral branch of the family, Mishari bin Abd al-Rahman. Turki's son, Faysal, defeated the usurper and succeeded his father.

In 1838, the Egyptians again invaded Najd, captured Faysal, and brought him back into exile for a second time to Cairo. (Faysal had been among the original exiles in 1818.) Muhammad Ali, who still had ambitions to extend his hegemony over the Arabian peninsula, placed Faysal's cousin, Khalid bin Saud, as amir of Najd in his stead. Khalid, a younger brother of the executed Abdullah, had also been exiled to Cairo in 1818 and was still residing there.

Khalid reigned as a virtual Egyptian puppet until 1840, when other foreign political reverses forced Muhammad Ali to withdraw his troops from Najd. The following year, Khalid was ousted by Abdullah bin Thunayan, who replaced him as amir. Abdullah was descended from Thunayan, a brother of Muhammad bin Saud and the founder of the Thunayan branch of the royal family.

In 1843 Faysal, who had escaped from Cairo, returned to Riyadh where he displaced Abdullah and again became amir. Faysal's second reign (1843–65) was to be the zenith of the Saudi state in the nineteenth century. Faysal and succeeding Saudi amirs were more often addressed as Imam than Amir. *Amir* is a secular title—the head of an amirate. *Imam* has a religious connotation. In this context, it means the leader of the *Umma*, or the Muslim community (that is, the "nation"). The term can also be used for the prayer leader in a mosque, a Muslim political leader, or (in Shi'a Islam) the leader of all Islam (that is, the "Hidden Imam").

The late historian R. Bayly Winder described Faysal, who adopted the religious title, as "farsighted enough to realize that he could not convert the whole world to Wahhabism, and that if he tried he would again bring ruin on his people and himself. He was a devout Wahhabi, but, instead of attacking Karbala, he received a British diplomat (Col. Lewis Pelly) in his capital."[5]

During Faysal's long reign, he restored order to Najd and expanded his domains north to the Jabal Shammar region and south to the frontier of Oman. He restored Saudi control over the Buraymi oasis, which the Saudis continued to claim although they again lost it in the late nineteenth century. The situation evolved into a major border dispute that was not settled until 1974.

Faysal's brother, Jaluwi, who was a loyal lieutenant, became the founder of another collateral branch of the family, the Ibn Jaluwis. For many years Ibn Jaluwis governed the Eastern Province of Saudi Arabia, and a number of Bint Jaluwis (*bint* is the female equivalent of bin or ibn) have married into the current ruling branch of the family.

Faysal's death in 1865 heralded another decline in Saudi fortunes. Two of his sons, Abdullah and Saud, were bitter rivals and constantly engaged in civil war. Abdullah was imam from 1865 to 1871, when he was ousted by Saud. Foolishly requesting help from the Ottomans, who had reoccupied the Hijaz after the death of Muhammad Ali in 1849, Abdullah was imprisoned by them for a few months. He escaped to reclaim power and was ousted again by Saud. After Saud's death in 1875, a third brother, Abd al-Rahman, claimed power but was ousted by Abdullah, who again became imam. When Abdullah died in 1889, he was succeeded by Abd al-Rahman.

While the Al Saud brothers were fighting among themselves, the state that Imam Faysal had restored began once again to collapse. In 1871, the Ottomans reoccupied al-Hasa in the east. In the south, Oman and the Trucial States (with British assistance) shook off Saudi rule, and in the north, Jabal Shammar revolted. Muhammad bin Rashid, amir of the Shammar, had served Imam Faysal as governor in the north from the Rashidi capital at Ha'il. By the time Abd al-Rahman became imam, Muhammad bin Rashid controlled nearly all of Najd and soon forced Abd al-Rahman to be his governor in Riyadh. After an unsuccessful attempt to challenge Rashidi hegemony in 1891, Abd al-Rahman fled in exile with his family to Kuwait, bringing the second Saudi state to an end.

ABD AL-AZIZ "IBN SAUD" AND THE CREATION OF SAUDI ARABIA

From humiliating defeat and exile, the Al Saud reemerged stronger than ever to create the third Saudi state, the present-day Kingdom of Saudi Arabia. The story of this extraordinary feat is largely the story of one man, Abd al-Rahman's son, Abd al-Aziz bin Abd al-Rahman Al Saud, known throughout the world as Ibn Saud.[6]

Abd al-Aziz (1876–1953) was an imposing figure of a man, well over six feet tall, handsome, with a commanding presence that caused other men naturally to gravitate to his leadership. What really set him apart from his contemporaries, however, was his breadth of vision—that innate ability to look beyond the immediate problems facing him and contemplate a future that his background and education did not really enable him fully to grasp. During his long political career, he successfully dealt with neighboring rulers, western diplomats, and oil executives alike. Although he did not live long enough to see his work reach ultimate fruition, he not only re-created the Saudi state but began the process that was to transform that state into the modern oil kingdom that is Saudi Arabia today.

The process of re-creating the Saudi state was not the irresistible tide

Figure 2.1. King Abd al-Aziz Ibn Saud, founder of the Kingdom of Saudi Arabia. Used by permission of the Saudi Information Office, Washington, D.C.

of success that it might appear to be nearly a century later. In the words of Philby, it was "the drama of a cause slowly but surely proceeding to its climax of final success through various vicissitudes of fortune, which now propelled it comet-like to the zenith, and now flung it headlong into the depths from which recovery seemed well nigh impossible."[7]

The first step in this process was to recapture the family capital of Riyadh from the Al Rashid. The story of this exploit is now legendary. In the winter of 1901, Abd al-Aziz set out from Kuwait with a handpicked band of 40 men, heading south and east into the desert. After spending some time in al-Hasa, he came up to Riyadh from the south in mid-January 1902. Splitting his force (which had grown to about 60 men), he proceeded toward the city walls, telling those left behind to make for Kuwait if they heard nothing from him in 24 hours. At the walls, he left 20 men under his brother, Muhammad, to await the signal of success or failure. With 10 men, he stole over the wall and broke into a house across the street from the al-Masmak fort, where the Rashidi governor, Ajlan, spent the night as a security precaution. Abd al-Aziz and his men waited for dawn, drinking coffee and reading the Quran.

In the morning, as Ajlan left the fort for his home, the invaders rushed his small party. Abd al-Aziz's cousin, Abdullah bin Jaluwi, threw a spear at Ajlan that missed and broke off in the fortress gate, where it remained for many years. Ajlan ran for the fort. After a brief struggle at the postern gate, he was killed by Abdullah bin Jaluwi, who then gained entrance to the fort. The garrison quickly surrendered, and the Al Sauds again became masters of Riyadh.

Abd al-Rahman, who had already decided that his son was better able than he to restore Saudi political fortunes, abdicated his claim to secular rule over Najd. However, he retained the more religious title, imam, which he kept until his death in 1928. Thereafter, no Saudi ruler has used that title. Abd al-Rahman remained a close confidant of his son, Abd al-Aziz, who consulted him constantly on matters of state and deferred to his senior rank on ceremonial occasions.

Following the recapture of Riyadh, Abd al-Aziz immediately set out to restore the allegiance of the Najdi tribes, relying on his personal charisma, political marriages (Muslims are allowed four wives concurrently), and the growing dislike of the brutal new Rashidi amir, Abd al-Aziz bin Rashid, who had succeeded his uncle, Muhammad, a few years earlier. Nevertheless, it took some 20 years for Rashidi power to be broken totally. Its downfall was in some measure due to rivalries within the Al Rashid family itself. Abd al-Aziz bin Rashid was killed by Saudi troops in 1906, but it was not until 1921 that Abd al-Aziz finally subdued the Al Rashid and captured their capital, Ha'il.

In order to defeat the Al Rashid, Abd al-Aziz realized that he needed more than the promise of plunder to keep the loyalty of traditionally fickle tribes. A firm believer in the Muwahhidin revival, he raised the banner of tawhid as his forefathers had done; but unlike them, he created a whole class of fanatical, ascetic Islamic warriors—the Ikhwan, or "the Brethren"—whom he settled in agricultural settlements located in Najdi oases. By 1912, the Ikhwan settler-warriors numbered 11,000. The following year, they wrested al-Hasa back from Rashidi control.

In the outside world, the creation of the third Najdi state was as unheralded as its two predecessors. Hardly anyone noticed when, in 1912, Abd al-Aziz elevated Najd from an amirate to the Sultanate of Najd and Its Dependencies in recognition of its increased size and importance.

But in the years leading up to World War I, Arabia again came into world focus. The British were seeking to counter rising German influence in the eastern Arab provinces of the Ottoman Empire, and Abd al-Aziz was seeking to counter Ottoman support for the Al Rashid. In 1910, Capt. W. H. I. Shakespear, the British political agent in Kuwait, informally contacted Abd al-Aziz and, in 1913, visited him in Riyadh while on a trek through Arabia.

British interest in central Arabia quickened on the eve of the war. In 1914, Shakespear was sent to Riyadh as the British political representative to Abd al-Aziz and was with him the following January when Saudi forces attacked the Rashidi forces at Jarab. After initial success, the Saudis were pushed back, and they finally broke in disorder. Shakespear, dressed in a British uniform and directing the fire of a single artillery piece, was killed. In December 1915, Abd al-Aziz met personally at Uqair on the Gulf coast with Sir Percy Cox, the new British political agent in Kuwait. There they concluded a treaty of friendship in which the British recognized Abd al-Aziz as the sultan of Najd and al-Hasa and gave him a small stipend.

In the wake of Shakespear's death, central Arabia ceased to play a prominent role in British war plans. The British focused instead on the Hijaz in western Arabia. In 1915, Sir Henry McMahon, the British high commissioner in Cairo, promised Sharif Hussein of Makkah that the British would support Arab independence if he would rebel against Ottoman rule. In June 1916, Hussein proclaimed the Arab Revolt, assumed the title "king of the Hijaz," and thereby became Britain's chosen instrument in Arabia. It was from the Hijaz that Colonel T. E. Lawrence (Lawrence of Arabia) launched his attacks against the Turks along the Hijaz Railroad running south from Damascus to al-Madinah.

Because both the Hijaz and Najd were allied with the British against the Ottomans during the war, Abd al-Aziz had refrained from hostilities against Sharif Hussein. Following the war, however, hostilities became virtually inevitable. Husayn was an ambitious man and, in leading the Arab Revolt, may have aspired to replace the Ottoman sultan as caliph of Islam. To Hussein, Abd al-Aziz was probably no more than another desert chieftain and a proponent of a dangerous and fanatical, if not heretical, religious revival movement in the bargain.

To Abd al-Aziz, a proud desert aristocrat and a devout adherent of the Muwahhidin revival, the worldly Hussein was hard to accept as custodian of the two holiest sites in Islam, Makkah and al-Madinah. Moreover, in 1912, Hussein captured Abd al-Aziz's brother, Saud, and released him only when Abd al-Aziz agreed to humiliating terms. Bad feelings also existed between the two leaders' sons. In 1919, Sharif Hussein's son Faysal snubbed Abd al-Aziz's son Faysal when they met in Paris as the Versailles Conference was in progress.

The first armed clash between the Saudis and the Hashemites occurred in May 1918. The Najdi Utayba tribal region on the frontier of the Hijaz was the source of friction. Hussein sent his son Abdullah (later king of Jordan) with an army to capture the Utayba town of Khurma. The Sharifian army was camped at nearby Turaba when the Ikhwan attacked and virtually annihilated it. An old Utayba tribesman who had been at the battle recalled 50 years later that only those with horses (about 100, including Abdullah) escaped. "Thank God I had a horse," he added, indicating for the first time which side he had been on.

Abd al-Aziz still did not press his advantage, but the Ikhwan were becoming more and more belligerent. Under Faysal al-Dawish, paramount shaykh of the Mutayr, they defeated Kuwaiti forces twice in 1920 and began raiding farther north. In 1921, after years of intermittent fighting, they finally occupied the Rashidi capital of Ha'il. To make peace with the Shammar tribes, Abd al-Aziz married the widow of Amir Saud ibn Rashid, who had been murdered by a cousin a year earlier, and adopted his children.

To prevent further border hostilities, Najd, Kuwait, and Iraq defined their common borders in 1922 in the Uqair Protocol, creating the Kuwaiti and Iraqi neutral zones. Far more than Iraq and Kuwait, however, the Ikhwan coveted the Hijaz and the holy cities of Makkah and al-Madinah. Moreover, Abd al-Aziz felt that he was being surrounded by hostile Hashemite regimes. Following World War I, Sharif Hussein had proclaimed himself king of the Arabs. The British had made one of his sons, Faysal, king of Iraq and another son, Abdullah, amir of Transjordan, both newly created countries with the status of British mandates. Amir Abdullah's growing relations with the Al Rashid was one reason why Abd al-Aziz finally annexed the Rashidi amirate in 1921. He had hesitated before then because of the political upheavals of World War I.

Even after the war he was loath to confront Sharif Hussein directly, as he was still an ally of the British. The final straw occurred in 1924. On March 3, Turkey abolished the caliphate, and two days later, Sharif (now King) Hussein proclaimed himself caliph of all Muslims. That was more than the Ikhwan could take, and Abd al-Aziz invaded the Hijaz. In August, the Ikhwan took Ta'if without resistance, but when a shot rang out, the ensuing melee resulted in a massacre of the inhabitants. The terrified Hijazis pressured Hussein to abdicate. His son and successor, Ali, whose control was by then limited to Jiddah, fared no better. In December 1925, he surrendered to the Saudis and followed his father into exile. In January 1926, Abd al-Aziz was proclaimed king of the Hijaz and sultan of Najd and Its Dependencies.

After several years of negotiating border agreements with British protectorate and mandate states, Abd al-Aziz finally gained international recognition in the Treaty of Jiddah, negotiated with Sir Gilbert Clayton and signed in 1927. The British recognized the new Saudi state, the name of which was changed to the Kingdom of the Hijaz and Najd and Its Dependencies. Although the new name implied a unitary state, Najd and the Hijaz continued to be ruled separately for a number of years—the latter administered by the king's second surviving son, Prince Faysal, who was appointed viceroy.

In 1930, Abd al-Aziz annexed Asir south of the Hijaz, which his son Faysal had taken in 1924. Yemen continued to contest Saudi sovereignty over Wadi Najran, on the Yemen-Asir frontier, until 1934 when it lost a brief war with the Saudis. Faysal and his older brother, Prince Saud, the heir apparent, commanded the Saudi troops. Abd al-Aziz asked for no further territorial concessions, but the resulting Treaty of Ta'if laid to rest the border dispute until it was revived again in the 1980s. Thus by 1930 Saudi territories were fairly well defined, with the exception of a few border disputes. The most important outstanding land border dispute was over the Buraymi oasis on the Saudi/Abu Dhabi/Omani frontier. Although the Saudis had not controlled it since Imam Faysal's day, they had not relinquished their claim. Saudi-British arbitration in the 1950s failed to settle the problem, but in April 1974 the Saudis finally gave up their claim in return for various territorial and other concessions.

On September 22, 1932, the name of the country was officially changed to the Kingdom of Saudi Arabia. Thus, in the space of 30 years, Abd al-Aziz, starting out from exile with a band of 40 men, had restored the Saudi patrimony. Although he did not know it at the time, he had also set the stage for the creation of the world's greatest oil power.

Even before the kingdom was fully consolidated in 1932, Abd al-Aziz realized that he would have to temper the militant zeal of the Ikhwan.[8] Following the annexation of the Hijaz and Asir and the demarcation of borders with Transjordan and Iraq, there were few battlefields left to contest. The Ikhwan became restless with inactivity and were even more discontented with the introduction of modern technology such as autos, airplanes, and telephones, which they considered the devil's devices.

Conditions got out of hand in 1928 when Faysal al-Dawish, paramount shaykh of the Mutayr, and other tribal leaders raised the banner of revolt and began raiding in neighboring Iraq and Kuwait, bringing British retaliation with airplanes and motorized infantry. A face-off with the king was inevitable and came in 1929, when warriors loyal to the king wiped out the rebels at the battle of Sibilla. Although modern aircraft (which

Figure 2.2. Modern petroglyphs of the battle of Sibilla, 1927, the last Bedouin battle in history. Used by permission of Timothy Barger.

Figure 2.3. Ancient petroglyphs in in Rub' al-Khali (Empty Quarter). Courtesy of Sebastian Maisel.

the king captured or acquired from the Hijaz and were operated by British pilots) and trucks were used, it was considered the last great Bedouin battle in history. The independent military power of the tribes was broken forever.

The Ikhwan was more or less disbanded, although tribal levies were again used in 1934 during the brief war with Yemen. In 1956, tribal warriors were organized into a paramilitary fighting force that became the nucleus of the present-day National Guard.

FROM DESERT KINGDOM TO MODERN OIL STATE

When Abd al-Aziz annexed the Hijaz in 1926, it had a more sophisticated government than Najd, which was ruled on a highly informal and personalized basis. The Hijaz had a Consultative Council (Majlis al-Shura) and a Council of Ministers (Majlis al-Wuzara; sing. *wazir*). The king left much of the Hijazi governmental machinery in place, and for many years it was used in public administration for the entire country. Major decisions, however, were made wherever the king was, mainly in Riyadh.

The first two national ministries were Foreign Affairs and Finance (later Finance and National Economy). The former was established in 1930 and headed by Faysal, who was also viceroy of the Hijaz. Faysal was to retain the position of foreign minister (with one short interlude) until his death in 1975. The Finance Ministry was created in 1932 and for a time undertook whatever other government tasks the king wanted done until separate ministries were created.[9] From this modest beginning, modern governmental institutions were gradually introduced until, shortly before King Abd al-Aziz's death in 1953, the government had so increased in size and complexity that the king established the Council of Ministers.

In the 1930s, the greatest obstacle to development was poverty. The kingdom was so poor that the finance minister, Abdullah Sulayman, kept the government accounts in a large black ledger that, it was rumored, he kept at home under his bed. Not only was Saudi Arabia one of the poorest countries on earth, but its economic situation was deteriorating as a result of the world depression and growing tensions leading to World War II. The major source of government revenue was receipts from the annual hajj, and with the worsening international economic and political conditions, hajj receipts had declined greatly. Oil was discovered in commercial quantities in 1938, but the kingdom was not able to exploit it because of the advent of the war.

It was not until after World War II that oil revenues began to be a factor in the economic and political history of the kingdom. During the war, the United States agreed to a lend-lease agreement with Abd al-Aziz to keep the country solvent when the oil companies, which had been advancing him monies based on future earnings, were no longer financially able to do so.

The history of Saudi Arabia since the war has been one of unprecedented social and economic development, funded almost entirely by oil revenues. So fast did development proceed that impressive projects of one decade were torn down and replaced by even more impressive projects in the next. Abd al-Aziz created a firm foundation for building the modern oil state that is Saudi Arabia today. It is doubtful that he fully understood the implications of the steps he was taking, but neither did the outside world. Becoming accustomed to the steady flow of relatively cheap Saudi oil, the world soon took the country for granted and turned its attention to other, more pressing matters.

Abd al-Aziz was succeeded by his eldest surviving son, Saud. (His eldest son, Turki, died in the influenza pandemic of 1919.) A well-meaning person and an able politician in the traditional desert mold, Saud was unable to cope with the growing complexities that oil wealth and rapid modernization created. His reign was characterized by palace intrigue, large-scale corruption, and waste. Despite unprecedented oil revenues, the kingdom was virtually bankrupt.

In 1958, King Saud was pressured into naming as prime minister his half-brother Faysal bin Abd al-Aziz. Faysal, who was the heir apparent and had been foreign minister since 1930, took over the reins of government and began both fiscal and administrative reforms. In 1960 Saud again took over the government, and Faysal retired to private life. It became increasingly evident, however, that Saud's mismanagement was threatening the viability of the kingdom. By October 1962, Faysal was being urged by many Al Saud members and religious leaders (the Ulama) to accept the kingship. But he declined, citing his promise to his father to support his half-brother Saud.

In 1962, Faysal became prime minister for the second time, with his half-brother Khalid as deputy prime minister. In many ways, 1962 was the beginning of a continuity of government that has lasted to the present day. Faysal appointed two half-brothers, Fahd and Sultan, as ministers of the interior and of defense and aviation, respectively, and a third, Abdullah, as commander of the National Guard. Among the more prominent and able technocrats appointed in 1962 was Ahmad Zaki Yamani, who as minister of petroleum and mineral resources played a major role in the kingdom's coming of age as a major oil power.

King Saud's pride made it difficult for him to accept the role of ceremonial monarch, and he repeatedly challenged Faysal in order to regain full governing powers. Finally, in late October 1964, the Al Sauds, supported by leading religious leaders, forced Saud to abdicate. The religious leadership issued a *fatwa* (a binding Islamic legal opinion) proclaiming Faysal king. Saud held on to power briefly, but on November 3, 1964, he abdicated and left Riyadh for the last time. A sick and broken man, he died in Greece in 1969.

If King Abd al-Aziz was the creator of the modern Saudi state, King Faysal was the architect of the modern oil kingdom.[10] The current trends in Saudi economic and social development and domestic and foreign policies all began during his reign.

His experience in foreign affairs began with an official visit to England in 1919 when he was 17. On his way home, he visited the Versailles peace conference. He was also, with a two-year hiatus, Saudi Arabia's foreign minister from the creation of the ministry until his death, and he attended the San Francisco conference creating the United Nations. As king, he attended Arab summits and made official visits to the major capitals of the world. With this background, he was always comfortable in dealings with both his Arab neighbors and the world at large. His preference was quiet diplomacy, but he could be punitive when he believed it was necessary.

Faysal also was formidable in his grasp of Islamic law, the constitutional basis of the regime. His mother was an Al al-Shaykh, and from her family he became so well versed in Islam that ultraconservative figures who attempted to oppose his modernization policies on religious grounds found that he knew more about holy law than they did.

Perhaps the most notable aspect of Faysal's reign was his ability to gauge just how far and how fast he could nudge his people toward modernity without exceeding a pace they could assimilate. He was also committed to preserving an Islamic society in Saudi Arabia and maintaining an Islamic political system. This careful approach often frustrated westerners who wished to see Saudi Arabia transformed overnight into a representative democracy.

Faysal recognized the need for evolutionary change of the Saudi political system, but he was in no rush to import alien western political ideologies or institutions. In 1962, he issued a 10-point political reform plan, largely in response to requests by President John F. Kennedy. As time passed, the U.S. government, seeing little progress in implementing the plan, instructed successive American ambassadors from time to time to raise the issue of political reform with the king. During one such démarche made in the late 1960s when American antiwar riots were rampant, the king replied by asking the ambassador whether the United States really wanted the kingdom to be turned into another Berkeley campus.[11]

Faysal was killed in 1975 by a deranged nephew, Khalid bin Musaid. At the time of his death, he was easily the senior statesman of the entire Arab world and a recognized world leader. He was succeeded by his half-brother, Khalid bin Abd al-Aziz. The new king was a pious, introspective person who lacked his predecessor's flair for government. Preferring to keep a low profile, he delegated much of the day-to-day running of the government to his half-brother, Prince Fahd, the new heir apparent. There was virtually no change in government policies and programs, and most of the veteran cabinet members appointed by Faysal remained in office.

Because of the high visibility of Prince Fahd and other members of the government—both royal family and technocrats—Khalid's role as king has been somewhat underestimated by outsiders. Despite his retiring ways, he was still very much in charge and had a talent for arbitrating among rival princes and technocrats and maintaining a consensus on the direction the kingdom ought to take. He was also popular among the people, who respected him for his modesty and piety.

King Khalid was never in good health, and he died of a heart attack in June 1982. He was succeeded by Fahd in a smooth transition. Prince Abdullah, the head of the National Guard, was named first deputy prime minister and heir apparent.

Fahd brought to the office of king a great deal of experience. He was appointed education minister in 1953 and interior minister in 1962, an office he held until he became heir apparent in 1975. Like Khalid before him, Fahd maintained the kingdom on the same basic course established by Faysal and with much of the same leadership.

Fahd reshuffled the cabinet and retired many distinguished senior bureaucrats, a move apparently motivated by his desire to infuse the government with new blood. In January 1992 he issued the Saudi Basic Law of Governance, upgrading the governmental system to meet the challenges of modernization.

At the same time, he took care to preserve the link between state policies and Islamic precepts (see chapter 6.) The first article of the Basic Law states, "The Kingdom of Saudi Arabia is a sovereign Arab, Islamic state with Islam as its religion; God's Book and the Sunna of His Prophet, God's Prayers and peace be upon Him, are its constitution; Arabic is its language; and Riyadh is its capital." In October 1986, he assumed the title Khadim al-Haramayn al-Sharifayn, or "Custodian of the Two Holy Places" (that is, Makkah and al-Madinah), a reflection of the Islamic nature of the regime.

He also focused on the need to increase public participation. In early 1992, after a decade of deliberations, Fahd announced the creation of the Majlis al-Shura (Consultative Council). Although not an elective body, it

has rapidly created a place for public participation in consultation leading to consensus, which is the ancient institution for legitimizing government policy making (see chapter 6).

In foreign policy, Fahd followed the lead of King Faysal in seeking cooperation with western as well as moderate area states to address regional
Middle East problems. Radical Arab nationalism had lost its credence
after the Arab defeat in the 1967 Arab-Israeli war, and as heir apparent
and ultimately king, Fahd could be more active in regional affairs. In
1981, he offered the Fahd Plan for an Arab-Israeli peace. The Israelis and
the United States rejected it as contrary to peace negotiations up to that
time base, which did not address any of the Palestinian core issues, and
the Arab states rejected it as not sufficiently demanding enough. After
watering it down, the Arab League adopted it as the Fez Plan in 1982, but
it was by then a lost cause.

In the 1980s, the collapse of the Soviet Union heralded the end of the
cold war, which for almost 50 years was considered by Saudi Arabia to be
the greatest security threat to the Islamic way of life not only in the kingdom but throughout the Muslim world. It remained concerned about
regional threats, however, and its fears were justified in 1990 when Iraq's
president, Saddam Hussein, invaded Kuwait, threatening the rest of the
Arabian Peninsula as well. After initial reluctance, King Fahd welcomed
a coalition of Arab states and others led by the United States to counter
the Iraqi invasion, and in 1991 Operation Desert Storm was launched to
drive Saddam out of Kuwait.

COPING WITH MODERNIZATION IN A HOSTILE WORLD

Desert Storm was a unique event in that western imperialism was not
vented by radical Arabs as a protest to western participation. The Saudi
military acquitted itself very well, which made it a source of pride among
most Saudis, and the hubris created by victory created the feeling that national security had reached an all-time high. But to a great extent, Desert
Storm blurred the nascent rise of social dislocation and unsustainable
political expectations that had been growing throughout the region.

The root causes were rapid modernization and accumulation of great
wealth. The latter enabled the kingdom to invest in modern health care,
which in turn created a population explosion and a dramatic lowering of

the median age. Affluent young males lost their work ethic and, with it, a sense of self-fulfillment from pride of accomplishment (see chapter 3). In the 1980s, many young Saudis volunteered to fight the Soviets in Afghanistan, but after the war many felt more marginalized than ever and turned to militant Islamism to give meaning to their lives, spreading this solution to their pain to the next generation. In this way, they were drawn to terrorist groups, the most effective of which was Osama bin Laden's al-Qaida. Thus terrorism gradually became the greatest national security problem facing the country (see chapter 7).

Social dislocations extended beyond the terrorist threat, however. The stresses of modernization had a polarizing effect on the general population. There were those who pushed for more rapid evolution toward a type of open, secular society and the democratic political system found in the West. On the other hand, there were those who feared the pace of change would bring too much secularization and wished to return to the stricter social and political order of the past. Both King Fahd and his successor, King Abdullah, wrestled with keeping the balance between those two poles and maintaining economic and social development while resisting secularization.

Fahd became incapacitated by a series of strokes in 1995, and in 1996 he turned over the reins of government to his half-brother, Abdullah. The next decade was a difficult period for the kingdom in meeting the challenges of social change, economic and political expectations, and national security.

National security became the primary issue in the wake of the September 11, 2001, al-Qaida terrorist attack in the United States in which 15 of the 19 attackers were Saudis. There followed a massive expression of hatred from traumatized Americans against Saudis and Muslims in general, fueled by the U.S. Israel lobby and the Bush administration, the latter to gain domestic support for its punitive "Global War against Terrorism."

But the national security really became vital in the kingdom in May 2003 when terrorists attacked residential compounds, killing not only western expatriates but Muslims as well. Since then, the government has initiated a successful counterterrorism program, attacking and rounding up terrorists and rehabilitating young recruits back into society. It is not possible to eradicate all terrorist threats anywhere. But the Saudis have certainly reduced it to more manageable proportions.

When Abdullah became king in 2005 upon the death of Fahd, one of his major concerns was growing public sentiment for more participation in the political process. Adjusting to the challenges of the global economy and security, he initiated a reform process of the political and judicial system as well as the educational sector. The for some very slow process aims at a renewal and revitalization of the origin of Saudi rule: a balance of politics and religion for the sake not only of survival but also the strong, lasting impact of the country of the two holy places.[12]

Thus Abdullah has continued the evolutionary process of modernization without secularization begun by Abd al-Aziz and interrupted temporarily in the face of the national security threats of the first decade of the twenty-first century. It will be an ongoing task in which new challenges must be recognized as older challenges are met.

3

Tradition and Modernization

Islam and Society

For many people in the West and the Middle East as well, Saudi Arabian society is often associated with nomadic Bedouin tribes. They envision Saudi men as descendents of camel herders living in tents in the deserts and women as subjugated and forced to wear veils in public. Ironically, there is also a widely held perception of Saudi society as made up of very rich oil sheikhs and princes who lavishly spend petrodollars and live a luxurious lifestyle. Although both images represent a small modicum of truth, Saudi society is far more complex than either of those stereotypes imply. Basically it is a collage of centuries-old tradition and breathtaking modernization.

TRADITIONAL SAUDI SOCIETY

Saudi society has always been closed and conservative.[1] This is especially true in Najd, the political as well as geographical heartland. Due to central Arabia's isolation and insularity, Najdis have developed a high sense of ethnocentricity. Not only do they view Arabia as the cradle of Islam, but they also see Arabian tribes as the origin of the Arab race and Arabic as the language of God and God's people. They also view themselves as the center of their universe, not only because of their historic isolation but also because, unlike most of their Arab neighbors, they were never subjugated to western colonial rule and thus they never developed feelings of inferiority.

Although Saudi culture is imbued with Islamic values, and although Islam labeled pre-Islamic times *jahiliya* (age of ignorance), some of the core Islamic cultural values can be traced to ancient Mesopotamian,

Israelite, and south Arabian as well as northern Arabian societies. For example, women covering themselves as a symbol of modesty can be found in the Old Testament in the book of Ruth where Boaz placed the skirt of his cloak over Ruth.

Whether tribal or not, the extended family, including not only parents and their immediate descendents but paternal aunts and uncles and even distant cousins, was the basic structural unit of traditional society, and it remains so to this day. All traditional extended families were patriarchal, patrilinial (male bloodlines), patrilocal (from specific locales), endogamous (having close marriage ties within extended family), and polygamous.

Patriarchal in structure, all families hold elders and seniority in great respect. As in the West, lineage is recognized through the male line. To this day, married women retain their family name and do not take the family name of their husbands. Bloodlines are also very important. Many Arabian families trace their lineage back to pre-Islamic times. As noted in chapter 2, for example, those tribal Arabians with the purest bloodlines are considered to be the Adnanis, generally found in northern Arabia, who claim descent from Adnan, a descendent of Ismail (Ishmael), and Qahtanis, generally found in the southern Arabia, who claim descent from Qahtan (mentioned in Genesis as Joktan, a great-grandson of Noah).

Although all traditional Saudi families respect and follow Islamic law, honor and its opposite, shame, were and remain important determinants of interpersonal and group behavior. And since ancient times, group decision making, whether in the family, in business, or in government, has relied heavily on consensus (*ijma'*) based on consultation with designated elders (*shura*). As discussed below, that practice was incorporated in and sanctioned by Islam, and it still exists today.

Traditional behavior was and to a great extent remains contextual and highly personalized. Western cultures place a high value on rationality, particularly since the Age of Reason. Traditional Saudi culture is as capable of empiricism, but perhaps because of the omnipotence of God in Islam, determining causality can change with the context in which one views an issue. Likewise, because interpersonal relations are highly personalized, positions on issues can also change depending on whom one is speaking to. These tendencies have often led to misunderstandings in cross-cultural communications.

Rapid modernization has challenged many of these traditional Saudi social values. What is most extraordinary, however, is the resilience of traditional social values despite the advent of secular western social values that have inevitably followed rapid modernization. Saudi Arabia is the birthplace of Islam, and virtually all Saudis are Muslims. In addressing the degree and nature of social change, the place to begin is with the impact of Islam on Saudi culture.

One behavioral characteristic clearly linked to the kingdom's traditional Islamic culture is a pronounced sense of the inevitability of events. Based on the Islamic emphasis on the omnipotence of God's will, it is often expressed in the Arabic phrase *In sha'allah,* or "God willing." If God does not will something, it cannot possibly happen, including events in a person's life that might normally be considered within the realm of personal responsibility. To outsiders, Saudis sometimes appear to use this Islamic concept of God's will as an excuse to abdicate personal responsibility—for example, in meeting some obligation. It would be a mistake, however, to call into question the subordination of personal will to God's.

This characteristic has often been called "Islamic fatalism" and as such can denote passivity. Total faith in God's will can be quite the opposite, however, as evidenced by the fanaticism of Islamist extremist groups throughout the region, which are convinced they are instruments of God's will. Faith in the inevitability of God's will also enables decision makers to wait far longer than others might for a desired outcome. Patience is a watchword of Saudi politics.

Two other traditional Saudi cultural traits are associated with non-western cultures generally, not just Islamic cultures: compartmentalization of behavior and personalization of behavior. Compartmentalization (or atomization) of behavior is a tendency to view events from one single context at a time, not seeking to explore all the ramifications of how it might appear in other contexts. In an Islamic culture, it is reinforced by the concept that all causality is based on God's will. This reduces the necessity for different responses to a situation to appear consistent in different contexts. Although Saudi (and other Middle Eastern) decision makers are obviously no more prone to inconsistencies than anyone else, they do have a tendency not to focus on the possible impact of policy decisions on ancillary issues—for example, the economic impact of a political decision. It is common, therefore, for a single issue to elicit different and sometimes incompatible policy responses depending on the context or contexts in which it is viewed—such as national security, political, or economic interests.

Saudi behavior is also highly personalized. For example, personal rapport is the *sine qua non* of good political relations throughout the Middle East. Proximity to power begets power, and losing face is to be avoided at all costs. As a result, an elaborate system guiding interpersonal relations has evolved. For example, a Saudi response to a question will almost always be calculated more for its effect on the other party than as an indication of true feelings.

Personalization does not always equate with personal contact. In negotiating on substantive issues, most Saudis prefer to let subordinates work out the details, enabling the principals to confirm agreements already reached and ensuring that neither party loses face if negotiations fail. A senior Saudi official once said that it is not uncommon for a Saudi being considered for a high position to be approached first by his driver to find out whether or not he would be interested. If he says no, the matter will never be raised again (although if he says yes, he still might not get it).[2]

Another manifestation of this characteristic is a tendency among Saudis to avoid saying no to a proposal lest the other party lose face. At the same time, they will not agree to a compromise when they do not believe it is in their best interests to do so. In some cases, negotiations have dragged on for years over issues that the Saudis have no intention of acceding to, but they will not directly say so.

ISLAM AND SAUDI SOCIETY

It is impossible to gain an accurate understanding of Saudi culture and society, traditional or modern, without a basic understanding of Islam. Since its birth 1,400 years ago, it has had by far a greater impact on present-day Saudi society than any other single factor. Superimposed on traditional cultures worldwide, it is still the primary guide for social, cultural, and political as well as religious values and norms in Saudi Arabia, the cradle of Islam, and also throughout the Muslim world.

Islam was first preached in 610 by the prophet Muhammad, a native of Makkah (Mecca), who was born around 570, a member of the clan of

Bani Hashim of the Quraysh tribe. Arabia was then and still is a family-structured society, and the Quraysh were the dominant tribe of Makkah, which was an important trading post on the caravan route from southern Arabia to the Mediterranean Sea. The people of Makkah were successful merchants and businessmen, and so was Khadija, who first worked with Muhammad and later married him. She was also the first to accept Muhammad as a prophet and messenger of Allah, the one God. Muhammad's message of *tawhid*, the ultimate belief in one God, combined with his appeal to equality and social justice, earned him many followers and enemies alike. The struggle of unification and embracing of the new system lasted over two decades until Muhammad returned to Makkah and the holy shrine of the Ka'aba. It took more time for the tribes of Arabia to come along, but the benefits overwhelmingly outweighed the risks. The gradual adaptation of shared values began creating a body of unique Islamic Arabian beliefs, customs, and rituals.

Muhammad died in 632, and leadership of the Islamic community passed down to caliphs (from *khalifa*, successor). A schism arose in 661 following the murder of the fourth caliph, Ali ibn Abi Talib, a cousin and brother-in-law of the Prophet. The schism, which was between Sunnis and Shi'as, the two major branches of Islam, was initially political over who should succeed Caliph Ali. (The term Shi'a comes from Shi'at Ali, the Party of Ali.) Over the centuries, however, doctrinal differences have arisen between the two branches, primarily around the messianic Shi'a doctrine of a Hidden Imam whom Shi'as believe is in a state of occultation and will return at the end of time to create an ideal Muslim community. There are three main Shi'a sects: those who believe the twelfth Imam (Shi'a successor) is in occultation and will return at the end of time; those who believe it is the seventh Imam; and those believe it is the fifth Imam.

Most Saudis are Sunnis, and many Sunnis consider Shi'a messianism to be a heretical affront to the one all-powerful God. Yet juridical differences over Islamic law are relatively minor between the main Sunni schools and the Shi'a schools of jurisprudence, all of which were established in the early years of Islam. There are also several significant Shi'a communities. The largest community, Ja'faris or Twelvers, is found mostly in the Eastern Province; a community of Isma'ils or Sevener Shi'as is located in Najran and the surrounding area; and a community

Figure 3.1. The Haram Mosque during a present-day hajj. Used by permission of the Saudi Information Office, Washington, D.C.

Figure 3.2. The Haram Mosque, Makkah, in 1933. Used by permission of the Saudi Information Office, Washington, D.C.

of Zaydis or Fiver Shi'as is located in the Tihama near Jizan, adjacent to northern Yemen, which is also predominately Zaydi.

THE FIVE BASIC TENETS OF ISLAM

Unlike Christianity, which is basically a theological system, the basic tenets of Islam are very simple, being summed up in the "five pillars" of the faith. The central pillar, expressing the basic tenet of the faith, strict monotheism (*tawhid*) is expressed in the first and most important tenet, the shahadah (profession of faith): "There is no god but God, and Muhammad is the Messenger of God," or in Arabic, *La illaha illa Allah wa Muhammadun Rassul Allah*. All that is needed to become a Muslim is to profess belief in one God, stressing the sovereignty and universal dominion of the one God, and recognition that God revealed himself to the world through Muhammad, his messenger.

Thus the scope of Islam is all-embracing based on the idea that God is the creator of all things. While western societies take pride in the separation of church and state, Islam teaches that there is no division between secular and sacred. God's will is manifested in every aspect of human life. The term *Islam* itself means submission to His will. It also means peace with one's self and one's neighbors. For Saudis, anything less is unimaginable and would create divisions in core values, feeding anxieties and frustrations that can spawn hostile behaviors.

The other tenets are *zakat* (charitable giving), *salat* (five daily ritual prayers said facing Ka'aba in Makkah, considered the spiritual and geographical center of Islam), *sawm* (fasting from dawn until sunset during the lunar Islamic month of Ramadan), and as discussed later, the *hajj*, or great pilgrimage to Makkah. The two holiest celebrations in Islam come at the end of Ramadan, the Id al-Fitr (Feast of the Breaking of the Fast), and at the end of the hajj, the Id al-Adha (Feast of the Sacrifice), which is celebrated throughout the Muslim world.

Another tenet, sometimes called the "sixth pillar," is *jihad*. Often translated as "holy war," it is actually a much broader concept, referring to both the private and corporate obligation to encourage virtue and resist evil—albeit by force, if necessary. By calling for jihad, modern Islamic puritanical revolutionaries obviously emphasize the use of force. In Saudi Arabia, a nonmilitary manifestation of jihad is the government

Committee for Propagating Virtue and Suppressing Evil, often called the "religious police." The mission of its members (*mutawi'in*) is to ensure public compliance with the Saudi Arabian interpretation of Islamic cultural and moral obligations. But even when not institutionalized, all Muslims are obligated to strive to become better Muslims, the broadest, literal, and most common form of jihad.

SIGNIFICANCE OF THE HAJJ

Of the five pillars, the hajj is of particular significance to the holy city of Makkah, to the region of Hijaz where Makkah is located, and to the country as a whole. Sura (chapter) 3:96–97 of the Quran states, "The first House of Worship founded for mankind was in Bakka [Makkah] . . . and whoever enters is safe. And the Pilgrimage to the Temple [the hajj] is an obligation to God from those who are able to journey there."

The first rite of the hajj, performed prior to entering Makkah, is entering into *ihram*, a ritual state of cleansing and consecration. Since earliest times, special stations have been located outside where pilgrims traditionally perform ihram, but in the age of modern transport the rites are now as likely to be performed on an airliner. It begins with a declaration of intention to perform the hajj. Where possible, this includes ritual bathing (or washing) and cutting of nails and hair. (Women usually cut three locks, whereas many men shave their heads.) Once in the state of ihram, hajjis are not allowed to cut hair or nails or engage in sexual intercourse. They next don special ihram garments; for men these are white terry-cloth, seamless sheets, one around the lower body and one draped over the upper body. Women wear white robes but do not cover their faces. The instep must be uncovered but sandals may be worn, and umbrellas may also be used to ward off the harsh rays of the Hijazi sun. The hajj was designed for the worship of God, not for creature comforts. The pilgrims then say two ritual prayers; the second one, the talbiyya, is repeated throughout the hajj:

> *Labbayk Allahuma, labbayk!*
> (Here am I answering your call, O God. Here am I!)
> *Labbayka, la sharika laka, labbayk!*
> (Here I am. Thou hast no peer. Here am I!)

Inna al-hamda wal-ni'amata laka wal-mulk!
(Yea, praise and grace art thine and dominion!)
La sharika laka!
(Thou hast no peer!)

This chant can be heard repeatedly throughout the hajj. Unless one has witnessed it, if only on Saudi television, it is difficult to capture the feeling of excitement and expectation as one voice soon becomes thousands of voices spontaneously chanting in unison.

The pilgrim is now ready to enter Makkah. For those who have saved for many years and traveled from half a world away, the experience can be the highlight of a lifetime. Pilgrimages to Makkah and even many of the rites of the hajj existed before the time of Muhammad. As a native of Makkah, Muhammad was certainly familiar with these rites, and as he began to preach God's new revelation, Islam, they became incorporated into the new religion.

Islamic tradition links the site to Adam, who is credited with building the first Ka'aba, a dark, rectangular stone structure that stands in the middle of the Haram Mosque. References in the Quran link it also to Ibrahim (Abraham) and Ismail (Ishmael), who are credited with building the present structure. According to legend, the Angel Jibril (Gabriel) brought to Ibrahim a stone that had stood on a nearby mountain since the flood, Jabal Abu Qubays. This is the famous Black Stone built into the eastern corner of the Ka'aba. The stone is said to have originally been white but turned black through contact with the sins of mankind. Tradition also has it that it is the site of sacrifice where, according to Islam, Ibrahim offered to sacrifice his son Ismail. Linking the hajj to Ibrahim and Adam, however, should not be construed as an attempt to increase the authenticity of the hajj. Seen from the Muslim perspective, the hajj is a duty, not because of tradition but because it is the will of God.

When the hajjis arrive in Makkah, they perform two rites, the *tawaf* and the *sa'y*, which together constitute the *umrah*. The umrah may be done without performing the hajj rites proper, in which case it is called the little pilgrimage in contrast to the hajj, or great pilgrimage. It does not, however, satisfy the Islamic obligation to perform the hajj.

The initial or arrival tawaf (*tawaf al-qudum*) consists of seven circumnavigations around the Ka'aba. Each year, just before the hajj, it is covered with a heavy black silk cloth with golden embroidery, called the *kiswa*. Following the arrival tawaf, many pilgrims attempt to kiss the Black Stone, encased in a silver frame on the side of the Ka'aba. Due to the crowds, however, only the strongest can get near. One may also drink from the holy well of Zamzam. Tradition has it that God created the well by striking a rock to provide water for Hajar (Hagar) and Ismail when they were about to die of thirst as she searched for water.

Adjacent to the original site of Haram Mosque and now a part of the mosque complex are two small hills, al-Safa and al-Marwa, about 400 meters apart. The sa'y consists of seven one-way trips between them to commemorate Hajar's search for water. Up to this point, pilgrims may observe the rites at will. Some enter ihram in advance, do the rites, and temporarily exit. To complete the hajj, however, all must have performed the arrival tawaf and be in the state of ihram.

On the eighth of Dhu al-Hijjah, excitement begins to mount. On that day the Ka'aba is washed down, and there is a special *khutbah* (sermon) delivered at the Haram Mosque. Then all who have not already departed head eastward out of town to the Plain of Arafat. There, on the ninth of

Figure 3.3. Modern hajj tent city near Arafat. Used by permission of the Saudi Information Office, Washington, D.C.

Figure 3.4. Jabal al-Rahma on Standing Day. Used by permission of the Saudi Information Office, Washington, D.C.

Dhu al-Hijjah, the climax of the hajj arrives, *yawm al-wuquf* (Standing Day). The wuquf lasts from noon to sunset and each hajji must be standing on Arafat at sunset for Maghrib prayers or the entire hajj is forfeited. It is a time of unmuted excitement. Arafat has become a huge tent city, and masses of people stretch as far as the eye can see. The preferred location is Jabal al-Rahma, the Mount of Mercy, which rises some 60 meters from the floor of the plain on the eastern side. It is so covered with white ihram garments that its stone face and thorn bushes can barely be seen. Everywhere is heard the chanting of the talbiyya. In the cryptic words of tradition, the wuquf is the hajj—the supreme hours.

Following sunset prayers, hajjis begin the *nafra,* the "Rushing," sometimes called the *ifada,* or the "Going Forth," in which everyone begins the trek back east to Mina, where they will do the final hajj rites and celebrate the Id al-Adha. The terms *nafra* and *ifada* have both become understatements, as all hajjis begin the trek at roughly the same time from the same place with the same destination. About 8 kilometers on the way is the small town of Muzdalifa. There, each hajji is encouraged to say evening prayers, and special grace can be obtained by praying at

Figure 3.5. Modern hajj stoning rite at Mina. Used by permission of the Saudi Information Office, Washington, D.C.

the roofless mosque called al-Mashar al-Haram (Sacred Grove). There is another wuquf and sermon that night at Muzdalifa. Afterward, they continue onward to Mina, some 9 kilometers farther.

On the first day at Mina, they begin the *rajm*, the ritual of lapidating or stoning. At the far end of town are three stone pillars, called *jamaras*, representing *shaytans* (satans). Seven stones are thrown on that day at the Jamarat al-Aqaba, and seven stones are thrown at the other two, Jamarat al-Wasta and Jamarat al-'Ula, over the next four days. After each stone, the hajji usually recites the *takbir*, "*Bismallah, Allahu akbar* (In the name of God; God is Great). Those too infirm to throw the stones (or unable to push through the crowds) can delegate another to do so for them.

The Id al-Adha lasts from the tenth through the twelfth of Dhu al-Hijjah and is celebrated throughout the Muslim world, where it is a joyous occasion characterized by visits from friends and relatives. During the Id, each family sacrifices an unblemished animal—generally a sheep or a goat but sometimes a baby camel. It is also permissible to sacrifice a

Figure 3.6. Hajj stoning rite, 1953. Used by permission of the National Geographic Society.

small fowl such as a pigeon, but most hajjis, after going to all the expense of making the hajj, spurn such animals.

The lapidations begin the de-sacrilization from ihram. For example, after stoning the first jamara, a pilgrim no longer recites the talbiyya. Following the sacrifice, the hajjis perform the final de-sacrilization rites. The first is generally a ceremonial haircut (cutting three hairs will do). Then everyone returns to Makkah to perform the *tawaf al-ifada* (the closing tawaf), although partaking of Zamzam water and performing the sa'y may also be done. Hajjis are then free from all ihram restrictions and return to Mina for the rest of the Id al-Adha.

On the thirteenth of Dhu al-Hijja, after the final lapidations, the hajjis prepare to leave Mina for the last time. Returning to Makkah, they perform the *tawaf al-wida'a* (the farewell tawaf). With that, their hajj has been completed, and each participant is qualified to use the formal title "hajj" or "hajji."

Most hajjis who have not already done so, however, journey on to the second of the two holiest cities of Islam, al-Madinah, 450 kilometers to the north. In 622, Muhammad and his followers fled to al-Madinah from mounting persecution in Makkah. Many chapters of the Quran were written there, and Muhammad's tomb is located inside the great Prophet's Mosque there. The flight, known as the Hijrah, marks the beginning of the lunar Muslim calendar (11 days shorter than the solar calendar), and Dhu al-Hijjah is the last month in the Hijria (Islamic) calendar year.

In sum, the hajj is unique in its pure size and scope and in its atmosphere of joy and pious devotion. In December 2008, the number of hajjis was 2.45 million, of which 757,000 were Saudi nationals, plus another 600,000 to 1 million without permits. As such it is unrivaled as a sacred religious act, the significance of which is seldom reported by the western media. On the contrary, the western media often accentuate negative events, such as administrative breakdowns and politically motivated demonstrations.

Certainly, there have been such incidents. Two major disruptions that got wide coverage were the seizure of the Grand Mosque in 1979 by Juhayman al-Utaybi and several hundred followers demanding political, religious, and economical change in the kingdom, and the violent demonstrations of Iranian pilgrims in 1987. But when considering the millions of pilgrims at the hajj with any western city of like size, such incidents are few indeed and have not undermined the joy and piety that pervade the annual event. And for Saudis, it remains above all a deeply religious experience for which they feel deeply honored to be host to those millions of the faithful who perform it each year and responsible for their safety and welfare while they are carrying out their religious obligations. So seriously does the country take this responsibility that the late King Fahd added to his title "Khadim al-Haramayn al-Sharifayn" (Custodian of the Two Holy Places).

ISLAMIC LAW AND SAUDI SOCIETY

Islam is basically a legal system, more like Judaism than like Christianity, which is mainly a theological system. Islamic law, or Shari'a (literally, "the pathway to the source"), is a complex system of regulations that in addition to Islamic theology forms the framework of living a healthy Muslim life. As such it is a primary area of specialization by Islamic scholars. Despite theological differences among the various sects of Islam (for example, between Sunnis and Shi'as), Islamic law is universally respected by all Muslims. The sources of the law are the Quran, the Sunna (a compendium of recognized traditions handed down from the prophet Muhammad and his companions [earliest converts] and compiled in the Hadith), *ijma'* (consensus of the Muslim community), *qiyas* (analogy), and *ijtihad* (inspired independent reasoning). Many Sunni schools of jurisprudence believe that the time for ijtihad is over, but the Hanbali school, which is predominant in Saudi Arabia, does not.

Many of the strictures found in the Quran and the Sunna, the primary source for Shari'a, are elliptical and in the early period of Islam required interpretation. That produced several different schools of jurisprudence (*madhab*, pl. *madhahib*). Sunni Muslims follow four recognized schools: Hanafi, Maliki, Shafi'i, and Hanbali. The Hanbali school, which is the most conservative and most literal of all schools on personal family law, is the predominant school in Saudi Arabia. Some Saudi religious scholars follow other Sunni schools, notably the Shafi'i Madhhab in the west and the Maliki Madhhab in the east; the Shi'a community in the Eastern Province follows the major Shi'a school, the Ja'fari Madhhab, and some Saudis along the Yemeni border follow other Shi'a schools, prominent in the Yemen.[3]

Shari'a is considered divine, all-encompassing, and unchangeable. Islamic legal theory asserts that the Quran is the literal word of God and that there is no justification for further legislation or a legislative branch of government as there is in western political systems. Nevertheless, all judicial systems must have contemporary regulatory and enabling codes. This is also true among those based on Shariʿa, particularly on issues on which there is no mention in the law.

Saudis are legally bound by the Shariʿa. Unlike western law in which acts are either legal or illegal, the Shariʿa includes five categories for the acts: *wajib*, acts that are obligatory; *mandub*, acts that are recommended and will bring reward but for which omission will not bring punishment; *makruh*, acts for which avoidance brings reward but commission does not bring punishment; *haram*, acts that are prohibited; and *mubah*, acts that are not specifically addressed in the Holy Law and about which it is indifferent.

As with virtually every facet of Saudi society, politics, and economics, the Saudi judicial system has evolved from procedures that were little changed since the advent of Islam into ones that must deal with modernization. In 2007, the Saudi judicial system underwent a major reform intended to make it more efficient. It is important to note, however, that Islamic law itself cannot be changed in any way and remains the basis of all Saudi jurisprudence.

ISLAM AS SAUDI POLITICAL IDEOLOGY

Throughout history, political movements have associated themselves with both religious and secular ideologies to provide a higher moral justification for whatever methods they have chosen to obtain their political agendas. Every major religion contains passages calling for both tolerance toward one's neighbor and peaceful relations among political entities and other passages that justify confrontation and the use of lethal force, both in the name of divine prophecy. Depending on where the emphasis is placed, religious political ideologies (and secular ones as well) can range from passivism to religious warfare. For example, the three major monotheistic religions—Judaism, Christianity, and Islam—have all spawned religious political ideologies at both ends of the spectrum over the centuries if not millennia. Within human memory there are both pacifist and militarist ideologies in each sect, and with no exception all have engaged in terrorist activities.

As noted in chapter 2, the political ideology of the Saudi regime since its founding in the eighteenth century has been based on the teachings of Shaykh Muhammad bin Abd al-Wahhab, the founder of the puritan, fundamentalist Islamic reform movement of Wahhabism. The reform movement was more intellectual than political. Its central focus was on strict monotheism (tawhid), complemented by condemnation of any false innovations to the fundamentals of the faith (bid'a) since the time of the prophet Muhammad.

Under the leadership of Amir Muhammad bin Saud, the message of tawhid began to resonate throughout Najd. One could make a case that the rapid growth of the conservative fundamentalist Islamist reform movement appealed to a conservative Najdi society, but Ibn Abd al-Wahhab's being driven out of Uyayna by his neighbors demonstrated that conservatism alone was not sufficient.

For a political ideology to resonate, several factors must converge, and Islamic cultural affinity with Wahhabi precepts is only one of them. A second factor is political leadership. For there to be followers, there must be a strong leader. Amir Muhammad bin Saud had the vision to want to unite the constantly warring Najdi tribes under the banner of tawhid. A third factor is a predisposition of potential followers to want to follow. For Najdi Bedouin tribes, intertribal (and intratribal) warfare had been a way of life throughout recorded time. They were also at least nominally Muslims. What resonated for them was that the Wahhabi reform movement raised their warring tribal way of life to a high religious cause.

Muhammad bin Saud, amir of the small desert town of Dir'iya, was won over to the reform movement, and this created a synthesis of temporal power carried on by his descendents, the Al Saud (House of Saud), and spiritual power represented by bin Abd al-Wahhab's descendents, the Al al-Shaykh; this has sustained political and social cohesion until today.

FROM ISOLATION TO GLOBALIZATION: MODERNIZATION, NOT SECULARIZATION

No facet of the evolution of Saudi Arabia from a desert principality to a major oil kingdom has been as vivid as the pace of social change. Until the early twentieth century, Najd, the political as well as geographical heartland of present-day Saudi Arabia, was one of the most physically isolated places on earth. Even the Hijaz, which had hosted pilgrims to the hajj from all over the Muslim world for centuries, had relatively limited contact with the western world.[4] But, because of Arabia's isolation and insularity, people have developed a high sense of ethnocentricity. Saudis truly believe that their Islamic culture is vastly superior to western cultures.

The fact that intensely conservative Saudi society has its Hanbali legal system and its Wahhabi political ideology does not mean that Saudi Arabia ever opposed modernization per se. With the advent of the oil age, the kingdom quickly absorbed western technology, accepted western creature comforts, and took a liking to many aspects of western pop culture. Nevertheless, so deeply ingrained were traditional Islamic Saudi social and cultural values that coming face to face with secular western cultural values was a shock. Dealing with cultural aspects of modernization has probably been the overriding challenge and the cause of much of the stress experienced by old and young alike.

King Abd al-Aziz, who could be called the father of modern Saudi Arabia, was both a devout Wahhabi and an extraordinarily farsighted ruler. He quickly saw the inherent incompatibilities between western secular values that inevitably accompanied modernizations and the deeply conservative Islamic values of his people. His response was to adopt a strategy still followed today that could be summed up as "modernization, not secularization." It was his opinion that preserving the fundamental teachings of Islam was not incompatible with technological modernization and that it was possible for the kingdom to maintain peaceful coexistence with the modern secular world. This vision was made a reality under Abd al-Aziz's son, King Faysal (reigned 1964–75), who could well be called the father of Saudi modernization. Faysal, whose mother was an Al al-Shaykh, was well versed in Islam and the precepts of the Wahhabi revival and was uniquely qualified to maintain the delicate balance between modernization and Islamic traditional values.

The more accessible that western creature comforts have become, however, the more traditional Islamic social values have collided with western secular social values. The result has been an increasing polarization within the society. On the one hand, there are those, particularly among younger generations, who are impatient with the evolutionary social policies and who call for more rapid social change. On the other hand, there are those, old and young alike, who are fearful of rapid social change and wish to push the clock back to the time of the prophet Muhammad.

A major area of stress is gender relations. It is widely believed in the West that Saudi women are subjugated to men, but that is not really true. Islam teaches that the sexes are equal under God. Traditional Saudi culture practices a distribution of labor going back to ancient, pre-Islamic times in which women were paramount in the home as nurturers and homemakers and men were paramount outside the home as protectors and providers. To this day, women predominate in the home, up to and including arranging marriages for their children. The person who might give a young bride the hardest time in her new home is her mother-in-law, not her husband. Recently a young Saudi woman was having trouble persuading her husband 'to enroll their son in a more challenging school against his will; the father took the son's side. When it was suggested to her that she appeal to her husband's father, she replied, "No, I'll call his mother; she will make him give in."[5]

Outside the home, however, women traditionally have had limited mobility beyond perhaps meeting with other women in one of their homes. Even today their mobility outside the home is restricted. For example, they cannot drive automobiles, nor can they travel outside the country without permission or being escorted by a male member of their family. Thus, while modernization has brought Saudi women more opportunity outside the home, expectations have risen even faster than opportunities. At the same time, winning mobility outside the home has come at the cost of exercising as much power in the home.

THE IMPACT OF MODERNIZATION

The benefits of modernization to Saudi society have been huge. But with the rapid introduction of so many modern public and private innovations, there has also been social cost.

Modern Medicine and Social Change

One of the greatest benefits to the kingdom has been the introduction of modern medicine and health care. Prior to the late twentieth century, modern medicine was virtually unknown outside of the Hijaz. And as with so many other aspects of modernization, the coming of modern medicine was itself an evolutionary process. It was first introduced in the Hijaz in the nineteenth century in conjunction with sanitation needs of the hajj, particularly the spread of cholera from the Far East to Makkah and then transmitted by hajjis from North Africa to Europe and on to the United States.[6] As a result, acceptance of modern medical practices in the Hijaz was far more widespread than in other parts of the country.

Modern health care was first introduced to the Gulf coast by American missionary doctors residing in Bahrain who were invited in 1913 by the then Saudi amir of al-Hasa (now the Eastern Province) to provide medical services for his people. They later provided services in Najd, including to Abd al-Aziz, although they initially met resistance from those who did not wish to abandon their traditional medical practices.[7] When the oil men employed by what was later named the Arabian American Oil Company (Aramco) arrived in the 1930s, they established their own company medical facilities. The missionaries, however, continued to provide services in the Eastern Province until they were phased out in 1955.

Although the kingdom was dedicated to offering modern health care to all its citizens, it was not until the rapid rise in oil revenues in the wake of the Arab oil embargo in the 1970s and 1980s that public and private modern health care became widely available throughout the kingdom.

Despite the great and obvious benefits that modern health care has provided, however, there has also been a social cost, primarily in the demographics of the country. One unforeseen consequence has been the rate of population growth. Given the huge size of the country, Saudi Arabia still has a relatively small population, and for many years rapid population growth was considered a good thing. It is becoming increasingly clear, however, that rapid population growth can have serious long-term consequences.

Before the oil era, Saudi Arabia, like many premodern cultures, particularly in unhealthy environments, traditionally had a high birthrate to compensate for the high infant mortality rates due to primitive health care. Families produced many children in order that those who survived could care for them in their old age. But with the advent of modern health care, infant mortality has been greatly reduced. And because basic cultural habits do not change rapidly, the birthrate has not declined at a commensurate rate.

The result has been a major population explosion over the last 40 years. Saudi Arabia now has one of the highest birthrates in the world, estimated at over 3 percent a year. By 2002, the median age had reached an estimated low of around 15 but has risen slightly since then. Even with a rising birthrate, however, it will take years for population growth to decline substantially. As the younger generations reach childbearing age, the Saudi population could double again in the next quarter century.

A related unforeseen demographic cost has resulted from the sharp increase in life expectancy. And again there has been an unexpected consequence for both young and old, males and females. Traditional Saudi society has always accorded respect to its elders, and they dominate family, business, and government administration and decision making with a minimum of delegation of authority. With the lengthening of life expectancy, however, the elders are living longer but are loath to turn over the reins to the next generation. This has not only stunted upward mobility and increased the marginalization of younger generations, but has also resulted in burnout and a loss of vision for the future. Moreover, the next generation have little chance of taking over from their elders until they themselves are well past middle age.

This has raised what many Saudis and western economists have seen as a related problem. With the vastly increasing numbers of Saudi males reaching adulthood, statistics seem to indicate that there are increasingly far more job seekers than jobs available. The Saudi government is well aware of the problem. The late King Fahd responded by placing tenure limits on senior government officials. The government also encouraged a "Saudiazation" policy to replace more expatriate managerial, vocational, and technical employees with qualified Saudis.

Sudden Wealth on Social Change

Affluence based on expanding oil wealth has undermined the work ethic for many younger Saudis who were raised to expect their wants and needs to be provided by their families. In traditional Saudi culture, males had to work hard to provide for their families in order to survive. But work was never linked to a moral work ethic such as other societies developed. As a result, many young Saudi men have become disinclined to accept junior jobs requiring hard work or else their level of productivity is too low to compete with foreign workers willing to work harder for far less pay. Despite the statistics, therefore, there are still employment opportunities available for young men willing and qualified to work hard and earn advancement. Thus Saudiazation, despite its positive intent, has not been as successful in the Saudi private sector as hoped. There is a danger, therefore, that in the long run, an increasing number of young Saudis might become economically marginalized and forced to increase their dependence on families for support beyond their capacity to provide it.

The younger generations of Saudi women, on the other hand, tend to have a much greater work ethic than men. They work harder, prepare themselves educationally, and are more willing to accept the challenges of a competitive career. The scope of professional careers is obviously much smaller than that of men, but they do have a special niche as doctors, teachers, and even stockbrokers working exclusively with other women due to the traditional separation of the sexes outside the family. And although they still generally see marriage and motherhood as women's highest calling, working mothers are becoming an increasingly important segment of the workforce.

Urbanization and Social Change

Urbanization poses another major challenge to the preservation of traditional cultural values. Until very recently, the country has never had a single metropolis. Riyadh did not become the capital until the early nineteenth century, and a century later it was still basically a large town. With a few exceptions, it was closed to western residents until the 1970s. In the 1960s, Mike Ameen, the Aramco representative in Riyadh, could invite the entire American community of Riyadh to his home to celebrate the Fourth of July. In the pre-oil era, the major cities—Makkah, al-Madinah, and the port city of Jiddah—were all located in the Hijaz and were involved mainly in providing services for hajjis. By the end of the 1960s, only about 26 percent of the population lived in urban centers. Jiddah had a population of only around 250,000; Riyadh had around 200,000, Makkah had around 100,000, and al-Madinah had around 60,000.

Thus before modern urbanization most of the Saudis lived in small to medium-sized towns or were nomadic. They were mainly engaged in agriculture and animal husbandry. Settlement patterns were linear and spread out, but everyone knew exactly where his family's home was located. Saudi society was traditionally shaped around a symbiosis of different lifestyles: nomadic, rural, and urban. Mutual support provided means of stability and survival. Although political power emanated mainly from the villages and oases of Najd, desert Bedouins and merchants from the few urban centers contributed to and benefited much from its unilateral nature.

In sharp contrast, an estimated two-thirds to three-fourths of the population is now urban. Most live in three major urban areas: Jiddah-Makkah-al-Ta'if in the Hijaz, Riyadh in Najd, and the urban areas of the Eastern Province, all near the oil center of Dhahran, including the cities of Dammam, al-Khobar, and al-Jubayl, suburban towns of the nearby al-Qatif Oasis, and the villages clustering around the large town of Hufuf in the great Hasa Oasis. The population of Riyadh, now the largest city, is approaching 5 million, and Jiddah's population is over 3 million.

Urban migration has cut off a growing number of people from traditional support systems. Nuclear families moving to the cities have neither the mobility nor the proximity to relatives and close friends that provided support systems in small towns and villages. While the more affluent often live in extended compounds of multiple nuclear families, poorer families often do not have that option, greatly increasing personal and marital stress and forcing new patterns on daily living. As more and more people are located in cities and large towns, extended family ties will inevitably weaken. Endogamous marriages, a traditional source of strengthening tribal and family ties, continue to decline. Thus far, traditional family values have tenaciously held on, but it will be a challenge to maintain them into the distant future.

Modern Education on Social Change

Adapting Saudi Arabia's traditional educational system to meet the needs of modernization has been one of the most difficult of all the transitions it has had to make. Traditional education was basically religious and took place in Islamic schools (sing. *madrasa*, pl. *madaris*). The educational requirements placed on modern education, on the other hand, are predominant secular.

That might appear to some to pose a conundrum for the kingdom's commitment to its policy of "modernization, not secularization." In fact, it has not been. Saudi culture and indeed virtually all Middle Eastern cultures have always placed a high value on education. The Saudi government has not only created universities in the kingdom with western curricula; it has also sent thousands of students abroad to complete their higher education. The real challenge is not the modern curriculum but rather the traditional pedagogical philosophy of Islamic education emphasizing rote memorization that has resisted change.[8] This is not to imply that memorization is undesirable per se, but rather that to prepare and educate students to meet the challenges in a modern world they must be taught to think rigorously, analytically, and objectively.

When modern education first began to evolve in the kingdom, there was virtually no one with a university education, and merely obtaining a diploma guaranteed a good job. But with thousands of college graduates and, as noted above, more young people of working age than jobs, that is not enough. The government is well aware of this conundrum and is seeking ways to address it. One popular way is partnership with western universities in programs located in the kingdom.

Modern Transportation Communications and Social Change

Other products of rapid modernization that have had a major effect on the kingdom have been the rapid advances in transportation and communications. Modern transportation has provided mobility never experienced before. The first modern means of transportation were closely associated with the hajj. Beginning in the nineteenth century, steamships began to transport hajjis to Jiddah, the port city for Makkah. In 1900, construction of the Hijaz Railway between Damascus and al-Madinah was begun under the Ottomans to transport hajjis overland to the Muslim holy land. Rail transportation was begun in 1908, but halted in 1916 during World War I when the section from Ma'an to al-Madinah was destroyed and never rebuilt.[9] Although motorized transport was introduced after World War I, there was no all-weather road system until after World War II. Limited air transportation was also introduced after World War I, but regularly scheduled air service inside the kingdom did not occur until after World War II. By the 1960s, international and domestic air service was in operation, bringing the world to Saudi Arabia and introducing Saudis to the outside world. An all-weather road system was also begun but not completed for another decade. The first long-distance highways went from Dammam and Dhahran to Riyadh and from Makkah and Jiddah to al-Madinah. The impact of mobility created by modern transportation on Saudi culture is virtually incalculable.

On the other hand, the impact of modern communications technology has been even more spectacular. As noted above, traditional communications were highly personalized and remain so today. A tradition still popular, particularly among older men, is weekly male group gatherings, or *shillahs*, where relatives, colleagues, and friends come together on weekends to play cards, smoke *shisha* (waterpipes), discuss business and the news of the day, and trade views. Shi'a men have similar albeit more religiously oriented group gatherings called Husayniyas. Women also get together in regular social gatherings.

The expansion of electronic communications throughout the twentieth century (telegraph and telephone) and mass media (radio and television) expanded the scope of available news and views. Government regulations regarding content for local print and electronic media have always created credibility problems. The greatest breakthrough in the expansion of private communications, however, has resulted from the information technology (IT) revolution. The advent of satellite telecasting has virtually rendered censorship obsolete. And the internet and cellular telephones have brought instant, affordable, person-to-person communications around the world to nearly all Saudi citizens, young and old.

Modern communications have restored the role of nuclear and extended families as the major source of personal support for members scattered all over the kingdom by urbanization or living abroad. Family members in the kingdom speak daily with relatives, no matter where they might be. They also provide a far broader source of information from around the world than might otherwise be available.

Modern communications have also enabled Saudis to conform to the letter of restrictive traditional social norms while adopting more modern behaviors. For example, in Saudi society, marriages usually have been arranged between the two families, and in the past, particularly in Najd, future spouses rarely met before the wedding day unless they were from the same extended family. However, the concept of young people meeting each other has been transformed due to the introduction of e-mail and cell phones. These are tools to facilitate new ways of interaction, where young people can get to know each other first and then arrange meetings between their mothers, who have traditionally taken the lead in arranging marriages.

SOCIAL MODERNIZATION AND TRADITION: A BALANCE SHEET

Saudi modernization made possible by oil revenues has brought many material benefits including unprecedented financial affluence, enhanced creature comforts, a high literacy rate, and the latest medical advances, communications, transportation, and information technologies. Forty years ago, virtually all food, clothing, and other marketable goods were negotiated in open *suqs* (markets). In the 1960s, there were still only two "mom and pop" groceries, one hotel, the Haramayn, one substandard hospital, and one family restaurant on the outskirts of town in Jiddah, then the country's largest city. There was only one modern institution of higher learning, the Petroleum and Minerals College in Dhahran. Now there are over 30 modern institutions of higher learning, and shopping malls, supermarkets, luxury hotels, and family restaurants are found in all major urban areas in the country.[10]

These benefits have not been without a price. Culture shock has had a polarizing effect on Saudi society between those who call for more rapid change and those who want to turn back the clock. But one thing is clear. The evolutionary nature of change that the kingdom has experienced thus far has been due in large part to the stabilizing effect of its cohesive society and its Islamic culture. By and large, Saudi society has faced this with equanimity.

The greatest achievement of Saudi society in modern times has been its ability to adapt to rapid social change through evolution rather than revolution. King Abd al-Aziz and his successors have preserved traditional values while encouraging modernization. The success they have had, however, has accelerated the pace of social change creating additional future challenges.

The challenge is not to prevent the collapse of the family as the major structural unit of Saudi society, nor is it to preserve traditional Islamic values. Core social and moral values do not change rapidly. The challenge is to maintain equilibrium in the face of rapid social, economical, and political change. Moreover, such equilibrium is not based on social, economical, or political conditions per se, but rather on unsustainable and unmet expectations resulting in fears and grievances that are the first steps toward hostility and unrest.

The focus must be on the heritage passed on to the younger generations. And one of the greatest threats to them is demographic: the population explosion and how it will affect the ability of young people to both create and maintain expectations from their extended families, which still command their first loyalty and are the first place they go for support and encouragement. Extended families, not the government, are still the bulwark of social order and thereby of economic and political stability. But if rapid population growth continues unabated, its role as the mainstay of the stable society that Saudis have long enjoyed will be in jeopardy.

Likewise, the oil revenues that rapidly transformed Saudi Arabia from a subsistence society to one of great wealth have also been a mixed blessing. Overindulged young men supported financially by their families have adopted increasingly unsustainable expectations for the creature comforts to which they believe they are entitled without the need for hard work. This could have adverse social and economic consequences for young people who lack a work ethic and self-discipline to be competitive in a free market economy.

All of these are potential long-term problems and have not presently reached a critical level. The extended family is still the anchor of a stable traditional but rapidly changing social system. But the longer that we postpone addressing these problems, the more difficult it will be to deal with them.

4

Oil and Saudi Arabia

Saudi Arabia is the quintessential oil state. As of 2009, it had approximately 265 billion barrels of proved oil reserves, estimated to be about one-fifth of the world total. Its productive capacity is approximately 12 million barrels a day (mbd), the world's largest. Oil export revenues accounted for an estimated 90 percent of total Saudi export earnings and state revenues and over 45 percent of the country's gross domestic product (GDP).[1]

With these figures, it is easy to see why Saudi Arabia is perceived as the quintessential Arab oil kingdom. Far 'more difficult to realize is that just a few decades ago it was one of the poorest countries on earth. The story of how a remote desert principality developed into a modern oil kingdom begins at the turn of the twentieth century, before the creation of Saudi Arabia itself.

MAKING OF AN OIL KINGDOM, 1901–45

On May 28, 1901, William Knox D'Arcy, a British financier who had made a fortune in gold mine speculation in Australia, concluded an oil concession agreement with the shah of Persia. It made Great Britain the preeminent oil power in the region for two-thirds of the twentieth century. From the concession emerged the Anglo-Persian Oil Company, later renamed Anglo-Iranian (AIOC), and ultimately British Petroleum (BP).

The oil business was far different then than it is today. The petroleum product in greatest demand in the nineteenth century was kerosene. Together with natural gas, it was used for heating and cooking and in the industrial world for lighting. Just when Thomas Edison's invention of the incandescent light bulb in 1877 appeared to deprive petroleum of its greatest long-term market, a new market opened up with the invention of the internal combustion engine. In the United States, in particular, this was to change the entire culture into one literally driven by the automobile.

The automobile age was still far off in the early 1900s, but oil-fired engines were finding other uses. One of the most momentous decisions for Middle Eastern oil was the British decision in 1912 to propel its navy henceforth by oil instead of coal. That almost instantly made Middle East oil a strategic commodity, and when War World I broke out two years later, the importance of oil was ensured.

Although the British pioneered in obtaining the first Middle East oil concessions, it was the Americans who developed Saudi oil resources. In the early years, however, the U.S.-Saudi oil relationship was far from a sure thing. Prior to World War I, the Americans, who were already the world's leading oil producers and were net exporters, showed little interest in obtaining foreign concessions. The war briefly spurred official interest in foreign oil as a strategic reserve, since its allies, cut off from their own sources, had become largely dependent on the United States.[2] The Middle East appeared to be one of the most promising areas for American companies.

Official U.S. interest in Middle East oil continued in the 1920s, not so much out of concern for strategic reserves as out of the desire to ensure that U.S. oil companies were not prevented by their European competitors from obtaining oil concessions. With strong government encouragement, seven U.S. oil companies created a joint venture called the Near East Development Company. The original companies were Standard Oil of New Jersey (Exxon), Standard Oil of New York (Mobil), Gulf, the Texas Company (Texaco), Sinclair, Atlantic Oil Company (now part of Atlantic-Richfield, or ARCO), and Pan American Petroleum (Standard Oil of Indiana). By the time of the acquisition, Texaco and Sinclair had dropped out and the shares of Pan American and Atlantic had been purchased by Standard of New Jersey and Standard of New York. Backed by the State Department, the joint venture obtained a 23.75 percent interest in the Iraq Petroleum Company (IPC) in July 1928.[3] The other owners of IPC were Anglo-Persian, Royal Dutch Shell, and French interests, each of which owned 23.75 percent. Calouste Gulbenkian, the Armenian oil man who before World War I had put together IPC's predecessor, the Turkish Petroleum Company, retained a 5 percent equity, for which he was nicknamed "Mr. Five Percent."

As it turned out, a far more important holdover from the old Turkish Petroleum Company was a self-denial clause, retained by IPC. This clause stipulated that none of the owners would undertake any oil operations in an area that included most of the former Ottoman Empire except in cooperation with the other owners. Gulbenkian later claimed that he redefined that area in 1928 by drawing a line with a red pencil around the defunct Ottoman Empire, including Asia Minor, the Fertile Crescent, and all of Arabia except for Kuwait. True or not, the clause became known as the "Red Line Agreement," and it included Saudi Arabia.[4]

By 1928, the sense of urgency to acquire foreign supplies had disappeared. Worldwide overcapacity and overproduction had become much more immediate problems. Many officials in both business and government feared that the financial stability of the entire oil industry could be jeopardized if the search for new markets were to lead to cutthroat competition and price wars.

Accordingly, in September 1928, just two months after the IPC agreement, the chief executive officers of Royal Dutch Shell, Anglo-Persian, Jersey Standard, Gulf, and Standard of Indiana met at Achnacarry Castle in Scotland, ostensibly for grouse shooting but in reality to hammer out a formula for limiting free competition and allocating market shares. The "As Is Agreement," as it came to be called, and the Red Line Agreement were among the first successful attempts to cartelize the international oil industry. Thus the motivating force behind creating an international oil cartel was not to raise prices, as was later popularly assumed, but to prevent prices from collapsing. With the onset of the Great Depression just a year away, the international oil cartel became even more of a myth as the oil companies desperately sought to expand their dwindling markets worldwide at the expense of their competitors.

As demand declined due to the Depression, and supply continued to expand with new finds, U.S. government interest in foreign oil supplies declined precipitously in the 1930s. Ironically, it was during this period that U.S. oil companies became established in Saudi Arabia. One could even argue that the lack of official support helped the companies more than it hurt them in obtaining a Saudi oil concession. Of all the competing companies, only those from the United States were not suspected by King Abd al-Aziz of being the precursor of imperial political interests.[5]

The Americans were not the first to be interested in a Saudi oil concession. In 1923, Maj. Frank Holmes, an entrepreneur and adventurer from New Zealand, obtained a concession for his Near Eastern and General Syndicate from Abd al-Aziz, then sultan of Najd, to explore for oil. Holmes was aided by a Lebanese American, Ameen Rihani. Although Abd al-Aziz was wary of opening up his country to foreign political exploitation, he was chronically in need of money, which an oil concession could provide, and he did not really believe that Holmes would find oil, a view commonly held by many oil geologists of the day.

Holmes was never really interested in searching for oil; he hoped to sell his concession to a company that was. He found no takers, and in 1928 the concession lapsed. In the meantime, he had negotiated another concession with the amirate of Bahrain, which he promptly sold to the Gulf Oil Corporation. Because Gulf was bound by the Red Line Agreement, however, it was not able to exploit the concession and sold it in turn to Standard Oil of California (Socal, now Chevron).

There was one more complication. Bahrain had signed an agreement with Britain permitting only British or British Commonwealth companies to explore for oil. Socal got around this restriction by creating a wholly owned Canadian subsidiary, the Bahrain Petroleum Company (Bapco), and in 1932, Bapco struck oil.

The Bahrain archipelago is located only 40 kilometers off the Saudi coast. (They are now linked by a causeway.) Finding oil so close to the mainland revived interest among Socal geologists in exploring for oil in Saudi Arabia, and with the help of H. St. John B. Philby and Karl Twitchell, Socal persuaded Abd al-Aziz to grant it an oil concession. Philby was a British army officer, diplomat, and adventurer who had met Abd al-Aziz on an official mission during World War I and had stayed on to become a close advisor. Twitchell was an American engineer who had previously surveyed Saudi water and mineral resources and was trusted by the king. The concession agreement was concluded in May 1933 and ratified by royal decree in July. In September, the first oil prospectors stepped ashore at Jubayl, now a major petrochemical industrial center and site of a Saudi naval base, but then only a village. In November 1933, Socal placed the concession under another wholly owned subsidiary, the Arabian Standard Oil Company (Casoc), the precursor of Aramco.[6]

Drilling commenced on April 30, 1935. The first well, called Dammam No. 1, and five subsequent wells were drilled to the same depth at which oil had been discovered in Bahrain, but the results were disappointing, with no oil found in commercial quantities. Thus, after Dammam No. 7 was spudded in on December 7, 1936, drilling continued below the Bahrain zone. On March 3, 1938, Dammam No. 7 began producing over 1,500 barrels per day—compared with between 5 and 10 barrels per day for many wells in the United States—and has done so ever since. Saudi Arabia had entered the oil age.

With world markets both politically and economically disrupted by the world economic depression and the deteriorating political situation leading ultimately to World War II, the 1930s were not the best of times for bringing new oil discoveries on stream. Thus despite the new discovery, the kingdom would have to wait for the end of World War II before any significant Saudi oil exports were made or revenues accrued.

In the meantime, Socal was endeavoring to negotiate with other oil companies to prevent a collapse in prices resulting from Saudi and Bahraini oil coming on stream. The problem was solved, not through negotiations, but by selling half-equity in both operations to Texaco. Texaco had overseas markets and almost no overseas oil, whereas Socal had few overseas markets and an abundance of overseas oil. In 1936, the two companies combined Near East and Asian operations, including Casoc and Bapco, under a jointly owned subsidiary named the California Texas Oil Company, or Caltex. Texaco in turn purchased half-interest in Casoc for $3 million, plus $18 million in deferred equity.

Unfortunately for Abd al-Aziz, the deteriorating political and economic conditions of the 1930s placed him in even greater financial straits than had chronically been the case. Saudi Arabia's economy depended primarily on hajj receipts, and as the numbers of hajjis dropped off, either from economic distress or because political conditions made international travel impossible, Saudi Arabia's financial situation was nearing collapse.

Initially, Casoc tried to keep Abd al-Aziz afloat through loans and advances on future revenues, but in early 1941, believing it could no longer afford to do so, Casoc appealed to the U.S. government to help bail out the king. Although the United States had not yet entered the war, many government officials believed that it would ultimately be drawn in, and interest in the strategic value of oil supplies was renewed. They were therefore favorably disposed to helping out the kingdom. Nevertheless, two years of protracted debate ensued within the U.S. government, plus U.S. negotiations with Saudi Arabia and Britain (considered the preeminent political power in the region) before help was on the way.

It took the form of a declaration on February 18, 1943, by the U.S. secretary of state, Cordell Hull, that Saudi Arabia was eligible for U.S. Lend-Lease assistance. By extending aid through the Lend-Lease program, which was justified on strategic military grounds, the United States not only ensured that Saudi Arabia would remain financially solvent during the war but also entered into military cooperation with the kingdom.[7]

As had happened in World War I, official U.S. interest in the strategic importance of Saudi oil soared during World War II, and also as previously occurred, it declined after the war. In 1943, U.S. Interior Secretary Harold Ickes recommended that the government purchase all, or at least part, of Casoc. There was certainly sufficient precedent in Europe for such a move, but in the United States, Cisco's owners opposed government equity on the grounds of traditional noninvolvement by government in private business. Nevertheless, the strategic importance of oil did convince both U.S. businessmen and public officials that some form of government involvement in foreign oil operations was inevitable. Casoc became the Arabian American Oil Company, or Aramco, on January 31, 1944.

The Birth of a Modern Oil State, 1945–50

The end of the war enabled Saudi oil finally to enter the market in significant quantities. And by 1948, U.S. government interest in Middle East oil had again waned, and it reverted to a policy of passive support for private U.S. companies operating in the region. Aramco's owners were left to work out for themselves such problems as market shares with their European and other American competitors. They became concerned about the effect of such an increase in supply on world oil prices. Fearing that the entry of so much oil on a glutted postwar global market could lead to price wars and a collapse of the entire market (a concern that had led to the creation of Casoc in the first place), they attempted to acquire additional partners with worldwide marketing operations that could distribute Aramco's production more widely.

The two most logical choices were Jersey Standard (now Exxon) and Standard of New York (now Mobil). Both had limited Middle East operations (they shared in the 23.75 percent American equity in IPC), and both had worldwide downstream (refining and marketing) operations. However, both were signatories to the Red Line Agreement prohibiting them from developing upstream oil resources in Arabia without sharing with the other signatories. With strong support from the U.S. government, the obstacles to the two companies obtaining equity in Aramco were overcome, including setting aside the Red Line Agreement, and in December 1948, Jersey Standard purchased 30 percent and Standard of New York bought 10 percent of Aramco. The two original owners, Standard of California and Texaco, each retained 30 percent equity.

There was still no thought on the part of the oil-producing countries to seek state ownership of their oil resources. Abd al-Aziz in particular wanted a wholly U.S. concession, which he thought would stick to being a commercial venture and not become an instrument of politics. The king never tired of seeking better financial terms from concessionaires, however. Thus, in 1949, he granted a concession to J. Paul Getty's Pacific Western Oil Corporation (later Getty Oil Company) in the Saudi-Kuwaiti Neutral Zone that gave the kingdom far better terms than it had obtained from Aramco. (The Neutral Zone had been created by the British in 1920 between the two countries to accommodate the Bedouins who roamed the area and for whom fixed boundaries made little sense. Both Kuwait and Saudi Arabia agreed to administer the territory jointly and to share oil production developed there.)

Coming of Age, 1950–73

In 1950, Saudi Arabia began to pressure Aramco for better terms as well. After intense negotiations, they agreed to 50–50 net profit sharing, with royalties and Saudi taxes being credited to the Saudi share. A major obstacle to the agreement was Aramco's fears that it would be subject to double taxation—both to Saudi Arabia and to the United States. This problem was overcome when the U.S. Treasury Department ruled that Aramco would be granted a tax exemption on the profit sharing, which in effect exempted the company from paying any U.S. taxes. The transfer of the tax liability to the United States was later cited by critics of the oil industry as a devious backroom deal, but there is no doubt that Aramco's owners took great pains to make sure that the entire agreement was drafted in strict accordance with U.S. tax laws.[8]

The Saudis were soon to do even better than 50–50, however. In 1957, a Japanese consortium, the Arabian Oil Company (AOC), was created to seek an offshore concession in the Neutral Zone. AOC agreed to a 44–56 split in the Saudis' favor, which was later increased to 43–57 when AOC agreed to those terms with Kuwait. Furthermore, when AOC discovered oil in 1960, Saudi Arabia and Kuwait took a 10 percent equity share in the company.

By 1967, Saudi Arabia was well established as a major oil producer. Yet, despite its growing wealth and status, it was one of the least known and least understood of the major oil-producing states. Events soon transpired, however, that were to make both Saudi Arabia and the Organization of the Petroleum Exporting Countries (OPEC) household words.

Despite Harold Ickes's dire warnings during World War II that the United States would become a net importer of oil, new worldwide postwar discoveries perpetuated a world market glut right through the 1960s. The major oil companies maintained price stability through collusion in regulating production rates.

When a soft market indicated that production cuts were necessary to keep the price of oil from collapsing, however, the revenues of the producing countries were reduced drastically. In 1960, Venezuela, twice stung by production cuts unilaterally imposed by the oil companies, sought to organize the producing countries to speak with one voice against such company decisions. Thus, in September 1960, OPEC was born. Saudi Arabia, which had also been stung, gave its full cooperation.

At the time, OPEC had virtually no influence over oil prices, in large part because the continuing oil glut perpetuated a buyer's market. Moreover, the producers were keenly aware of Iran's experience a decade earlier. In 1951, Iran, then the world's largest exporter, nationalized its oil resources in the belief that the world could not get along without its oil and, in a spate of antiwestern nationalism, did not offer due compensation to the concessionaire, AIOC. Unfortunately for Iran, there was more than enough oil production elsewhere to meet world demand, and in the resulting dispute over compensation with AIOC, Iran was forced to cease production until it reached a settlement with AIOC that was far more generous than the Iranians had wished. Moreover, it has never recovered its position as the number one oil-exporting nation.

The glut continued over the next two decades, and during that period, the producing companies seemed to hold all the cards. Nevertheless, with the creation of OPEC, the seed had been planted among the oil-producing countries that one day they would gain control over their own oil resources.[9]

Structural changes were taking place in the world economy at this time that would end the glut. Throughout the 1960s, world oil demand rose faster than supply. In Europe, industries were changing over from coal to oil at a rate faster than predicted, and in the United States, which was already the world's greatest oil consumer, cheap oil prices boosted demand even more. Oil consumption was also on the rise throughout the third world.

The end of the glut came in 1970, helped along by the fact that the United States had finally become a net importer of oil. The shift to a seller's market enabled the producing countries to supplant the oil companies in setting price and production rates and then to gain complete ownership over their own oil and gas resources.

In retrospect, the process actually began with the June 1967 Arab-Israeli war. By closing the Suez Canal, the war created a tanker shortage and placed a premium on Libyan crude that did not have to transit the canal and was also valued for its low sulfur content. In response, Libya demanded a price increase. Negotiations began in September 1969, the same month a group of Libyan army officers under Colonel Mu'ammar Qadhafi seized power. The Libyans concentrated on Occidental Petroleum, a small, "independent" U.S. oil company with few sources of crude outside Libya, and demanded that it agree to pay them higher revenues or face nationalization. Occidental tried to resist the Libyan demands by seeking alternative crude supplies from the major oil companies, but the majors, not realizing the folly of their actions, summarily turned down Occidental's request. It therefore had no alternative but to give in, and in August 1970 it signed an agreement giving Libya a 20 percent increase in oil royalties and tax revenues. By December, all the other companies in Libya, including major oil companies, were also forced to capitulate.[10]

The Libyan victory heralded a new era for international oil as other OPEC countries quickly demanded higher prices and tax rates. At a meeting in Tehran in February 1971, oil companies operating in the Gulf signed an agreement with their host governments agreeing to terms similar to those obtained by Libya. This agreement marked the transfer of control over oil price and production rate setting from the oil companies to the oil-producing countries in OPEC.

At the same time, the oil-producing countries were acquiring ownership of the oil resources that the companies had previously owned through the concession agreements. Most countries accomplished this by nationalization. Three countries—Saudi Arabia, Qatar, and the United Arab Emirates (UAE)—did so through "participation," a scheme first developed by the then Saudi petroleum minister, Ahmad Zaki Yamani, at a speech at the American University of Beirut in 1967. Yamani subsequently explained the participation idea to U.S. ambassador Hermann Eilts and some of his staff at a meeting at Yamani's summer house near Ta'if, Saudi Arabia. At the time, most oil industry experts dismissed the idea, not realizing the great changes in store in the next few years.

Yamani believed that direct nationalization of oil resources held certain disadvantages, including the negative political associations of punitive nationalization schemes. He also feared the prospect of cutthroat competition among the oil-producing countries for market shares, leading to a collapse of the market—the same fear that the companies had expressed at Achnacarry Castle some 40 years earlier.

As an alternative, he proposed allowing the companies to maintain equity in upstream production, during which time they would participate as partners in maintaining market stability. This concept was subsequently endorsed by OPEC in June 1968, and in July 1971 OPEC passed a resolution calling for its immediate implementation.

After extensive bargaining, Saudi Arabia, Qatar, and the UAE concluded participation agreements with the major concessionaires in late 1972. The kingdom acquired 25 percent ownership of Aramco early the next year and, in doing so, established control over Aramco company policy. It was therefore in no hurry to complete the process of buying out the company's equity. It increased its share to 60 percent in 1974 and finally to 100 percent in 1980. The new national oil company's name was changed to Saudi Aramco, and it is now the world's largest oil company.

The Arab Oil Embargo and a Period of OPEC Ascendency, 1973–80

As we have seen, market forces determine the price of oil in the long run, not political forces. When the oil glut of the 1950s and 1960s finally gave way to a shortage, it set the stage for the precipitous price rises of the 1970s. Within this broad economic context, however, short-term political disruptions did have a profound effect on the market. It was noted how the 1967 Arab-Israeli war created an oil tanker shortage that contributed to the transfer of control over oil production from the oil companies to the producing countries. The 1967 war was not the sole cause of the transfer of control, but it did serve as a catalyst, causing the transfer to occur sooner rather than later.

The 1973 Arab-Israeli war had a far greater disruptive effect on the market than the 1967 war, in the form of the Arab oil embargo. The Arab oil-producing states had attempted an embargo during the 1967 war, but there was still sufficient spare production capacity to make up for any shortfalls. By 1973, the oil market had changed completely, and with a world shortage, the oil embargo was extremely effective.

In September 1973, OPEC demanded higher oil prices in response to an increasingly tight market, and when negotiations with the oil companies convened in Vienna on October 8 to agree on a price, OPEC demanded a 100 percent increase. The companies, powerless to resist, broke off negotiations, and on October 16 the Gulf producers met in Kuwait and unilaterally raised posted prices 70 percent.

In the meantime, the 1973 Arab Israeli war had broken out on October 6. For almost a year prior to the war, King Faysal had been warning anyone who would listen that unless some progress were made on a Middle East peace settlement, the Arabs would be forced to use oil as political leverage to offset one-sided U.S. support to Israel. They believed such support enabled the Israelis to continue to deny Palestinians their right of self-determination.

When the war broke out, President Nixon personally assured Faysal that the United States intended to remain evenhanded during the fighting and to strive to establish a cease-fire. On October 19 Nixon asked Congress for $2.2 billion in military aid to Israel; two days later, Faysal declared the request to be not only gratuitous but a betrayal of the president's personal assurances to him. The following day, under the aegis of the Organization of Arab Petroleum Exporting Countries (OAPEC), Faysal instituted the Arab oil embargo.[11]

It had two parts: an absolute embargo on the United States and the Netherlands, considered especially friendly to Israel, and a cutback in production to ensure that the embargoed countries could not simply shift purchasing patterns for a fungible worldwide product—that is, increase imports from non-Arab sources whose customers would then increase purchases from Arab sources. To make it all work, the Saudis threatened to cut off supplies to Aramco's owners—four of the world's seven major oil companies—unless they geared their international supply networks to deny Arab oil to the Americans and the Dutch. The embargo was highly effective, and the artificial shortage it created was quickly exploited by OPEC price hawks led by Iran to again increase prices. At the December OPEC meeting, posted oil prices were raised another 130 percent.[12]

The embargo, which lasted until March 1974, was essentially an economic response to a political problem and should therefore be seen as political policy and not oil policy. In the United States, the embargo-induced oil shortage (exacerbated by inept U.S. policies) was met with surprise and outrage. In retrospect, no one should have been surprised that the Saudis and other Arab producers would attempt to extract a political price for U.S. Middle East policies considered by even moderate Arabs to be hostile to their interests and to use virtually the only form of leverage on U.S. policies that they had: oil.

Despite all the hysteria among consumer countries over the embargo, it had relatively little lasting impact on the Arab-Israeli problem other than to make the kingdom anathema to Israel and its supporters, who feared that the West and particularly the United States might "sell out Israel for a barrel of oil."

The embargo had a far greater impact on the oil market, exacerbating the oil shortage and resulting in high prices for much of the 1970s. The high prices in turn forced consumers to become more energy efficient and to search not only for other sources of oil but also for non-oil sources of energy. It also led to the creation of the International Energy Agency by major consuming countries in an attempt to work collectively to avoid another panic situation if oil were again used as a political weapon.

From the Saudi point of view, the embargo was not an unqualified success. With few natural resources other than oil and gas, the Saudis have always favored stable prices low enough to ensure a long-term market for their oil and to discourage shifts to nonfossil fuels. It has deviated from this policy only when short-term political or economic circumstances dictated. The 1973 Arab-Israeli war was such a circumstance. Ironically, the economic impact of the embargo was contrary to Saudi long-term economic interests. Not only did the embargo spur energy conservation and a worldwide search for alternative sources of energy, but the soaring oil prices of the 1970s, which enabled the Saudis to amass billions of dollars in foreign exchange, led to a deeper and longer glut in the 1980s that ultimately saw those reserves disappear.

Of far more importance in the short run, the Arab oil embargo underscored the completion of the process that had begun in the late 1960s whereby OPEC countries seized control of their own oil resources and acquired the ability to set price and production rates worldwide. Within OPEC, Saudi Arabia emerged as the uncontested leader. From a backward desert principality, it became the most important country controlling one of the world's most important commodities.

In many respects, very little of OPEC's successes in the 1970s was of its own making. OPEC was not a monolithic cartel, as it has been described. Its actions required unanimity, which was very hard to get. There was a fundamental split between "price moderates" such as Saudi Arabia, which had few other natural resources and saw their interests best served by moderate prices and long-term market stability, and "price hawks" such as Iran and Algeria, which saw their interests best served by high prices and high revenues to be used for rapid economic development.

What kept OPEC together, other than a strong desire by all its members, was the fact that most OPEC states were already producing at near capacity, and maintaining market shares was not a problem. The Saudis, who produced far more oil than their revenue needs required, could afford to raise or lower production to maintain price stability. Being the "swing producer" became a basic tenet of Saudi oil policy. Under their leadership, the absolute price of oil actually dropped during this period (i.e., the rise in prices was less than the rise in inflation). In late 1976, Saudi Arabia and the UAE even broke ranks with the rest of OPEC, increasing oil prices only 5 percent compared with 10 percent for the others. In the summer of 1977, the two countries raised their prices an additional 5 percent in return for a price freeze that was maintained until the end of 1979.[13]

By the summer of 1978, the Middle East was heading toward another political disruption of the oil market—the Iranian revolution. By December, it had become clear even to a previously optimistic U.S. government that the shah's regime was in serious trouble. When Ayatollah Khomeini returned to Iran from exile in February 1979, the end was in sight. He

Figure 4.1. Aramco oil installations at Shaybah in the Empty Quarter. Courtesy of Sebastian Maisel.

quickly organized an interim government and, following a plebiscite, announced the creation of an Islamic republic on April 1, 1980.

The psychological impact on the market of the fall of the shah was similar to that of the Arab embargo six years earlier, sending short-term "spot" market and futures market oil prices soaring. Fears that Iranian oil would stay off the market due to political upheavals were largely unfounded, but panic buying continued, further encouraged by strategic stockpiling. Having been caught with few strategic reserves in 1973, many countries and companies had planned extra storage capacity for just such another contingency. The added pressure that stockpiling had on oil demand helped drive up oil prices even higher, from around $25 per barrel in early 1979 to over $40 by mid-1980.

The Oil Glut, 1980–2003

In September 1980, the market faced yet another political disruption, the Iran-Iraq war. This time, however, the results were not the same as in 1973 or 1979. The price of oil was already inflated beyond its true market value, and worldwide recessionary trends were already beginning to lower prices. After a brief spike following the outbreak of the war, prices continued to decline. An oil glut was setting in that would last for a generation.

On the supply side, the seller's market of the 1970s substantially increased production, setting off a worldwide search for oil. High prices also made higher cost production more competitive. On the demand side, energy consumption decreased far more than anticipated. Not only had economic policies of major consuming countries stressed more energy conservation, but advances in fuel consumption technology greatly increased fuel efficiency. The increased availability of oil supply and reduced per capita consumption lowering demand accelerated the swing back to a buyer's market.

OPEC countries including Saudi Arabia had adjusted their national budgets to match their higher revenues, and when prices declined, they were politically unable to reduce their expenditures accordingly. To stabilize prices at a higher level, OPEC members agreed collectively to lower production in order to stabilize prices at a higher level, and Saudi Arabia, which assumed the role of "swing producer," agreed to the highest production cut. But OPEC could not maintain discipline over cutting production. The overwhelming temptation of other members was to continue to produce as much oil as possible, placing the burden on Saudi production cuts to prevent a price collapse. Saudi production dropped from 9.8 mbd in 1981 to a low of 2.34 mbd for August 1985.

Maintaining production cuts thus became untenable. Although they were confident that demand would eventually pick up, their revenues in mid-1985 were less than half of their budgetary expenditures. The kingdom thus increased production, both to force the other members to share the burden and to increase market share, and by 1986 prices dropped briefly in 1986 below $10 per barrel. In 1988, they again felt forced to increase production, and prices collapsed again. In short, the swing producer failed, and OPEC influence on the market remained at a low ebb for the next 15 years.

When Iraq invaded Kuwait in August 1990, oil prices again spiked but quickly fell after the Iraqis were expelled the following year. On balance, the economic burden of the war was a net burden to the Saudis due to the combined hard currency and budgetary costs to the kingdom in underwriting Desert Storm, which amounted to around $60 billion. As a result, they were forced to take the politically painful step of increasing foreign borrowing for the short fall.[14] Deficit financing, to which the government first resorted in the 1980s, continued until the end of the oil glut in 2003.

In sum, by avoiding really painful austerity measures throughout the oil glut, Saudi Arabia gambled that the glut would end before the kingdom exhausted the huge reserves it had amassed in the 1970s. To a degree, it lost the gamble, for the glut lasted far longer than expected. From 1985 to 2003, global aggregate oil prices when adjusted for inflation hovered around $25 per barrel.

The glut might have been over sooner if a number of major consumer countries had not begun to increase energy taxes. Energy taxes are not new, but Saudi Arabia and other producing countries became increasingly concerned that the wave of new taxes was designed primarily to transfer revenues to them from the producer states. For example, the European Community earned around $200 billion in taxes on about 10.3 mbd of petroleum products in 1991, compared with exporters' revenues of only $64 billion.[15]

In effect, the Europeans had become "swing consumers," damping demand by raising energy costs at home in the same way as Saudi Arabia sought to be a swing producer in the 1980s to regulate supply. It is possible that the glut could have lasted longer had the United States had the political will to levy higher taxes. But the overwhelming public consensus was that energy prices should always remain low and that the producing countries should raise production to keep it that way.

The Global Oil Price Spike and Collapse, 2004–2008

The glut finally came to an end in 2004. After years of excess supply, growing global demand finally surpassed global production. The shift was mainly attributed to China, but demand grew elsewhere as well. As national economies, particularly in China, India, and other Asian states, continued their rapid rise, demand outstripped supply, ending 23 years of cheap oil prices.

The rapid price rise was more complex than global market prices based on oil supply and demand would have created. There were other contributing factors to rising oil prices. For example, hurricanes in the Gulf of Mexico in 2004 and 2005 did extensive damage to offshore U.S. oil and gas rigs, further reducing domestic oil-producing and refinery output. As the United States was the greatest oil consumer and importer in the world, this also affected the global market. Another factor was short-term speculation in oil futures markets, driven in part by unfounded fears of the rapid decline in global oil production in many aging fields including those in Saudi Arabia. As a result of these and other factors such as renewed fuel efficiency due to higher prices and increased investment in alternative sources of energy research and development, prices rose beyond normal market levels. By mid-2008, aggregate prices had risen to more than $140 per barrel.

The buyer's market was initially a boon to Saudi Arabia. Years of deficit spending had eroded its earlier financial reverses, and expanding subsidized local consumption had lowered the level of available exports. As oil revenues grew, the country's financial situation rapidly improved. At the same time, Saudis feared that sustained high prices could reduce demand and oil revenues and encourage more rapid development of alternative energy sources. In June 2008, the Saudis announced plans to increase production and, if necessary, raise capacity to 15 million bpd.[16]

By the fall of 2008, however, the market collapsed. High oil prices contributed, but the main cause was the rapidly expanding global recession that began in the United States. The seller's market was over. By January, aggregate spot oil market prices were below $40 per barrel.[17] Yet by June 2009, prices had risen to over $70 per barrel.[18] The price fluctuation, however, was not caused by the fundamentals of global supply and demand; global demand remained low. Rather, it was apparently due to speculators buying oil on the futures market, betting that the recession was about to bottom out and that, in the wake of global economic recovery, demand would increase more rapidly than supply, creating an even higher spike in prices.

Looking to the Future

Before looking into the future, it would be helpful to review briefly the economic fundamentals of global oil economics and additional external factors that have influenced the market in the past and could well do so again in the future.

FUNDAMENTALS OF OIL MARKET ECONOMICS

The first fundamental is that with the invention and mass production of the internal combustion engine, oil has been a global commodity bought and sold in a global market. Thus where a consumer buys oil or where a producer sells it is irrelevant to the price. Prices are based on aggregate global supply and demand. The technical term describing such a commodity is *fungible*.

A second fundamental is that because it is a fungible commodity, oil prices tend to be cyclical. Prices for oil, which had long been cheap, began to climb when the United States first became a net importer in 1969, and prices soared after the Arab oil embargo further reduced supply. By 1980, however, high prices had induced increased global production, creating an oil glut that lasted until 2003. With growing world demand, prices again spiked, only to collapse again with the advent of the global economic recession in late 2008.

A third fundamental is that a major consumer or producer can temporarily influence market prices, but over time the market mechanism will readjust prices back to their true global market value.

External Market Influences

Among the external factors that could affect the global oil market are policies, punitive or benign, that are more politically than economically motivated. For example, King Faysal orchestrated the Arab oil embargo in the 1970s in response to what he considered a dishonorable breach of promise by President Nixon that the United States would be "even-handed" in the 1973 Arab-Israeli war.

Ironically, the rapid rise in oil prices that the embargo sparked was totally contrary to Saudi Arabia's long-held policy of price moderation. With their oil-based economy, the Saudis have feared that excessively high prices could lead to a premature global swing to nonfossil fuels. Equally ironic was that while the oil glut that followed resulted in more efficient fuel consumption, it also created a long period of deficit financing for the kingdom and higher global fuel consumption.

In addition, global economic conditions such as the global booms or recessions can also affect the oil market. For example, the collapse of oil prices in the fall of 2008 was caused more by the global recession that began in the United States than by high oil prices.

FUTURE PROSPECTS

As of 2009, the Saudi oil sector is still facing the major global recession. Despite many forecasts, no one can yet say with any degree of certainty how deep it will become or how long it will last before the global economy recovers. The EIA's Annual Energy Outlook for 2009 predicted "virtually no growth in U.S. oil consumption" because of new fuel efficiency standards, regulations requiring more renewable energy, and an assumed recovery of oil prices. In the longer run, the report predicts that demand will grow by about 2.5 percent a year between 2007 and 2030.[19]

The Saudis have already begun to address future prospects. Indeed, as a result of their economy's overwhelming dependence on oil revenues and the realization that it is a nonrenewable commodity, the Saudis have begun investing in long-term development of nonfossil fuels. They also insist that oil prices must be stabilized so that they can not only invest in productive capacity to meet future increases in demand but also invest in alternative renewal sources of energy.[20]

Meeting this goal will not be easy. Neither the kingdom nor OPEC can accomplish a relatively smooth transition to a new energy era alone. In any case, the kingdom will be obliged to engage in deficit financing until the recession is over (see chapter 5). If the global economy recovers in the medium term, the kingdom should be able to avoid a serious fiscal crisis. The longer recovery takes, however, the more difficult that will be.

The short-term challenge for the Saudi oil sector therefore will most likely be how to manage deficit financing until prices rise again. The medium-term challenge is likely to be to balance domestic fiscal requirements with needs for longer-term capital investment in fossil fuels while also preparing for an inevitable long-term development of alternative energy sources.

The long-term prospects are likely to be the most critical. Presumably, the current recession will keep prices low until the global economy begins to recover, reducing capital investment in expanding production. The long-term challenge for Saudi Arabia is not about running out of oil or other fossil fuels. They will ultimately be priced out of the market as supply declines. The challenge will be maintaining a comprehensive energy strategy that will diversify its overwhelming dependence on exporting fossil fuels.

The long-term challenge of making the transition to alternative sources of energy, of course, must be global in scope. Some global efforts are under way among consuming countries, but there is as yet still an insufficient sense of urgency or political will among producers alike to meet the global challenge. The worst-cast long-term prospects for the Saudi oil sector are therefore bleak. As the global economy recovers from the recession, low prices will stimulate new growth in demand, which in turn will create higher prices and a buyer's market, starting the cycle all over again.

In sum, short-term prospects for future Saudi oil production appear relatively somber but manageable. Medium-term prospects could well be a period of prosperity. The real challenge is a long-term creeping crisis as the transition to alternative sources of energy will be too little and too late to avoid economic, political, and social disruption. The least tractable dangers are climate change and the environmental costs of not addressing carbon emissions created by reliance on fossil fuels, which now make up 85 percent of all the global energy consumed. Saudi Arabia is well aware of the long-term threat to producers and consumers alike and is seeking ways to make the transition, such as investing in the development of nonfossil fuels. But this will require global cooperation. In the meantime, the longer the transition is delayed, the bleaker the long-term prospects for the Saudi oil sector and for the national and global economies as a whole.

5

Economic Development and Modernization

As are all facets of life in Saudi Arabia, the economic system has evolved from a traditional, mostly subsistence mercantile economy to a modern oil giant within living memory. As is true of other facets of life, the Saudi economic system remains subject to Islamic law.

TRADITIONAL SAUDI CAPITALISM

Desert capitalism has existed in Arabia since ancient times. Nomadic Bedouins practiced animal husbandry and traded livestock and protection to sedentary peoples in towns and villages in return for goods and foodstuffs they could not provide. Wherever water was to be found, in great and small oases and in the mountains inland from the Red Sea, crop irrigation was possible. From ports on the Gulf and the Red Sea, fishing, pearl diving, and maritime trading could be found.

A high civilization existed in south Arabia from the twentieth-first century BC until the fifth century AD. Saba (Sheba) was one of the ancient city states in what is now Yemen. Saba's wealth derived from its monopoly over frankincense and myrrh, which were only found in southern Arabia and Somalia and were highly valued for use in funeral pyres by the Romans before the spread of Christianity. A major trade route north through the Hijaz was dominated by Nabataean traders from their capital at Petra in present-day Jordan. Extensive Nabataean ruins can be found at Mada'in Salih north of al-Madinah.

Whether subsistence or high profit capitalism, behavioral norms evolved from ancient times that are still widely practiced today. These norms are easily recognizable to anyone who has frequented the suqs (markets) and bazaars of the Middle East.

The first and perhaps most important norm is *caveat emptor* (buyer beware), a governing principle of business negotiations since ancient times. The seller charges whatever the market will bear, and it is the responsibility of buyers to determine the fair market price they are willing to pay. There were no fixed prices until modern times, and a corollary associated with supply and demand is that the negotiating party that shows the greater degree of urgency to conclude a contract is likely to get the short end of the bargain. At the same time, it is not necessarily considered morally reprehensible to accept payment for services rendered that would be considered a conflict of interest or even graft in the West. No payment is due if no service is rendered, even though that does not prevent some from seeking unearned payments.

A second traditional norm is the high degree of personalization and degree of personal trust. As mentioned in chapter 3, it exists throughout the society, not just in business transactions. Thus the stranger is generally at a disadvantage unless he can establish a degree of mutual trust, preferably "eyeball to eyeball." The downside of personalization in business relations is extensive resort to *wasta,* a middleman, with influence that can help land a contract and/or influence the outcome of negotiations in one's favor.

ISLAM AND TRADITIONAL SAUDI CAPITALISM

Islam has always sanctioned free market economics, and although the Hanbali school of Islamic jurisprudence is notably conservative, it is one of the most liberal schools regarding business and commercial activities. It is no accident, therefore, that the kingdom has one of the most open free market economies in the world or that traditional Saudi business practices were among the most free-wheeling.

There are numerous measures in Shari'a for regulating contracts and commercial transactions. Probably the most stringent Islamic prohibition in free market capitalism is charging the ban on *riba,* generally interpreted as interest and/or usury. In pre-Islamic times, usurious rates for lending money or extending credit were the norm. Whether references to riba in the Qur'an banned usurious interest rates or all interest as a financial instrument, however, has been the source of much debate among Islamic legal scholars.[1]

In the early years of Islam, banning riba was not an insurmountable problem for commercial transactions in subsistence mercantile economies such as found in Najd. Thus domestic commercial banking was prohibited throughout the Saudi realm until the twentieth century, and financial transactions were negotiated through money changers.

Due to the hajj trade, however, the Hijaz had a far more sophisticated economy than elsewhere in what became Saudi Arabia. As the numbers of hajjis began to increase with the advent of modern transportation, particularly with the introduction of steamships in the nineteenth century, more sophisticated banking procedures were needed. Due to the Shari'a restrictions on financial services, colonial countries, particularly the Netherlands and Britain, began offering trading and financial service in Jiddah to the hajjis from countries under their colonial administration. The first foreign banking operations were maintained by a British trading firm, Gelatly Hanky and Company, which established a Jiddah branch in 1884.

Those Hijazis whose livelihoods were most directly linked to the hajj comprised the hajj service industry. Organized centuries ago into guilds that were quite similar to the medieval guilds of Europe, their general makeup has not changed greatly to this day. They consist of *mutawwafs*, who serve as guides for the holy rites in Makkah (Mecca) and environs; *zamzamis*, whose name came from their original function of providing hajjis with water from the holy well of Zamzam in the Haram Mosque in Makkah and who now assist mutawwafs in guiding hajjis; *wakils* (deputies of the mutawwafs), who meet and process hajjis in Jiddah; and *dalils*, who serve as guides in al-Madinah (Medina). There were others in past times, including *sambukjis*, who rowed hajjis ashore in small boats called *sambuks* from ships anchored in the outer harbors of the ports of Jiddah and Yanbu before there were adequate landing facilities.

Of even greater economic importance was the retail and *entrepôt* trade associated with the hajj. Until the mid-twentieth century, hajjis stayed longer, sometimes years, before returning home, and the bulk of retail commerce in the Hijaz occurred during the hajj season. Although oil revenues have long ago replaced hajj revenues as the backbone of the Saudi economy, the hajj season remains a major retail commercial season.

Virtually everyone in the Hijaz benefited in one way or another from the yearly influx of pilgrims to Makkah and al-Madinah. Hajj fees represented the major source of government income. In the private sector, the hajj brought commercial opportunities for the sale and resale of goods and services. Most of the great Hijazi merchant families, who for years formed the backbone of the Saudi commercial establishment, got their start in the hajj trade. Even the nomadic tribes of the Hijaz and western Najd used to benefit from the hajj, charging overland hajjis travelling through their areas for "protection." Indeed, under the Ottomans and the post–World War I Hijazi government, the hajj served as a great opportunity for Hijazi, Najdi, and northern tribes alike to shake down unsuspecting pilgrims for as much money as possible.

In addition to Islamic legal norms, two traditional Islamic cultural values also had an impact on traditional Saudi commercial and financial activity: attitudes toward work and wealth. With the traditional Islamic cultural emphasis on the belief that the source of all wealth is God's bounty, the population as a whole in what is now Saudi Arabia never developed a strong work ethic. Although most families, particularly those with a subsistence income, had to work hard simply to survive, they did not develop the sense that hard work was a form of seeking God's grace or that work simply for its own sake was morally uplifting.

Traditional attitudes toward wealth have also changed little and are substantially different from those in the West. Because wealth is considered within the dominion of God's creation, no guilt is attached to amassing private wealth. On the other hand, Islam teaches that as God provides wealth, it is incumbent on all who are recipients, public and private, to see to the needs of the less fortunate, not merely as an act of generosity but as a religious obligation, *zakat* (alms). Moreover, Saudi extended families, not the government, assume the primary responsibility for the financial welfare of their members. In addition, each individual is obligated to provide Zakat and the traditional system of private religious endowments for the poor, *awqaf* (singular *waqf*), administered through the Ministry of Islamic Endowments (Awqaf), Call to Islam (Da'wa), and Guidance Affairs.

Despite the central role that Islamic law has played in traditional Saudi capitalism, there is one area in which it could be said to have been somewhat less visible. That was in the sanctity of legal contractual obligations.

In the West, commercial disputes are generally subjected to litigation. In traditional Saudi capitalism, such legal obligations can be ignored in cases considered matters of honor. Moreover, in the traditional culture, time was not necessarily linear, and such disputes can drag on interminably. As will be discussed below, adapting to more litigious western business standards has evolved, but far more slowly than many western business executives might wish.

In sum, traditional Saudi capitalism had changed little since the coming of Islam when the twentieth century ushered in the oil era. Viewed from that perspective, the change has been little short of miraculous. Many traditional business ethics and practices survive, and the degree of change as the economy adapted to modernization has been highly selective. The most change to modern business standards has depended on the degree to which individuals, companies, and governments wish or are compelled to compete in a larger, now global marketplace.

THE EVOLUTION OF AN OIL KINGDOM

Despite free market capitalism and an egalitarian society, there was little distinction in the traditional economy between the public and private revenues. When Abd al-Aziz annexed the Hijaz in 1926, there was great fear throughout the Muslim world that he would apply strict codes of behavior for those making the hajj. In fact, quite the opposite was the case. He considered the hajj a religious obligation and went to great lengths to make sure they were dealt with fairly by the Hijazi hajj service industry, much to the consternation of the Hijazi merchant class.

The same year he annexed the Hijaz, the king allowed the Dutch to open the first commercial bank in the kingdom, the Netherlands Trading Society, located in Jiddah. For many years, the Dutch Bank, as it was called, was the only commercial bank in the kingdom. It also initially conducted most of the international monetary transactions for the kingdom.

Hajj income became the main source of revenue for the entire country, not just the Hijaz. The drastic reduction in the numbers of those making the hajj in the 1930s, due to the Great Depression and global political upheavals leading to World War II, pushed the kingdom to the verge of economic collapse. As mentioned in the previous chapter, this was averted only by advances on future oil sales by U.S. oil companies and during World War II by the U.S. government. Thus it was not until after the war that the transformation from a desert principality to a major oil kingdom really got under way.

FROM SUBSISTENCE TO AFFLUENCE

In the wake of World War II, oil revenues finally began to accrue in sufficient quantities to enable Saudi Arabia to cease living off foreign handouts for its economic survival. Even so, the evolution to a major oil economy did not occur overnight, and old mercantile attitudes persisted. Although the Saudi Ministry of Finance had been created in 1933, both public and domestic private financial institutions were rudimentary at best. Economic policy decisions were still made according to the highly personalized traditional system that had been in existence on the Arabian Peninsula for centuries. Paper money was distrusted, and none was in circulation. Financial transactions, including Aramco royalty payments, were made in specie, generally Saudi silver riyals and British gold sovereigns, although the Bedouin often preferred Austrian Maria Theresa silver thalers.

Most private sector banking was still carried on primarily through traditional money changers and branches of foreign banks. Even after the opening of modern banks, many locals continued to patronize the money changers in their picturesque stalls in the suqs (markets). Dealing in incredibly large sums, these traditional bankers kept up with the latest currency quotations worldwide and put their own money into the western commercial banks.

During the 1950s, foreign banks began to create branches. The British Bank of the Middle East opened a branch in Jiddah in 1950 and took over the accounts of Galatly Hanky in 1954. Gradually other western banks opened branches. The first Saudi domestic bank, the National Commercial Bank, was registered in 1953 by two prominent money changers, Abd al-Aziz al-Kaaki and Salim bin Mahfouz.[2]

In the years immediately following the war, the call for reforming the kingdom's finances grew among Saudis and westerners alike. The task was formidable. Public attitudes failed to distinguish between public and private revenues, believing that what God had bountifully bestowed on the country was there for the taking by any Saudi who could lay claim to it. Few Saudis were technically qualified to understand the complexities of government finance, including the aging King Abd al-Aziz and his finance minister, Abdullah Sulayman. Not only were public attitudes a hindrance to reform, but Islamic tradition, with its proscription on interest payments as usury, presented additional problems. Public distrust of paper money and banking in general stemmed from the association of both with usurious practices.

The influx of oil revenues—from almost nothing in 1945 to $57 million in 1950 and $340.8 million in 1955—required a vastly improved system for managing government monetary and fiscal affairs. Moreover, many foreign banks had established branches in the kingdom following the war, creating the further need for more comprehensive banking regulations.

Although the British and French made a number of recommendations for reforms, it was the Americans who were most involved in the early phases of creating modern Saudi monetary and fiscal institutions. With government finances in chaos, the U.S. Export-Import Bank loaned the kingdom $10 million in 1946 and another $15 million in 1950 to keep the government solvent. During the same period, partly in response to Saudi requests and partly on its own initiative, the United States began offering technical assistance.

In 1948, George Eddy, a gold expert with the office of international finance of the U.S. Treasury Department, and Raymond F. Mikesell, from the U.S. State Department, traveled to the kingdom to study currency reform. Saudi Arabia was then on a double standard, gold and silver, and market fluctuations between the two made maintaining a stable currency virtually impossible. The Eddy-Mikesell mission made recommendations but little headway. In August 1950, another U.S. mission, headed by John F. Greaney, arrived to help design an income tax (since abolished).

It was not until 1951 that major reforms got under way. In January, Saudi Arabia signed a Point Four technical assistance agreement with the United States that was to have a major impact on monetary and fiscal reforms. The following summer, a Point Four financial mission under Arthur N. Young arrived to help reform the budgetary and administrative system of the Ministry of Finance and improve the tariff system.[3]

It was in monetary reform that the Young mission made its largest impact, however, recommending the creation of a central bank. On April 20, 1952, the Saudi Arabian Monetary Agency (SAMA) was created. The term *monetary agency* was chosen in order to avoid mention of a bank or financial institution, which could carry the connotation of charging or paying interest. Charging and paying interest were specifically forbidden in the SAMA charter.

SAMA's initial charter listed its objectives as follows:

a) To strengthen the currency of Saudi Arabia, to stabilize it in relation to foreign currencies, and to avoid the losses resulting to the government and people from fluctuations in the exchange value of Saudi Arabian coins whose rates have not so far been fixed in relation to foreign currencies, which form the major part of the government's reserve;

b) To aid the Ministry of Finance in centralizing the receipts and expenditures of the government in accordance with authorized budget and in controlling payments so that all branches of the government shall abide by the rules.[4]

SAMA was also tasked with regulating the commercial banks and managing the kingdom's reserves.

The first two governors of SAMA were Americans, and the third was Pakistani. Thereafter, Saudis have managed what has become one of the most powerful central banking institutions in the world.

SAMA officially opened on October 4, 1952, and immediately embarked on currency reform. One of the first measures was to issue Saudi gold sovereigns, making the kingdom the only country at the time that had a fiduciary gold coin. Silver riyals were then pegged to the sovereigns at a ratio of 40 riyals to one sovereign. The sovereigns were withdrawn in 1954 because of a flood of solid gold "counterfeit" sovereigns from abroad, taking advantage of the higher price of the sovereign than its bullion equivalent.

Even more creative was SAMA's introduction of paper currency. SAMA's original charter prohibited it from issuing paper currency, due to local resistance and concern that it might encourage anti-Islamic banking practices. As a result, large transactions became very burdensome. With only one denomination of silver coin available to meet the monthly payroll, for example, Aramco had to purchase, transport, and store 60 tons of silver each month.[5]

Hajjis also had difficulty exchanging their foreign currencies for riyals and carrying around the heavy silver coins. In July 1953, SAMA began issuing scrip known as "hajj receipts" in denominations of 1, 5, and 10 riyals. Hajjis could exchange their currencies for the hajj receipts at any

Figure 5.1. Evolution of Saudi currency. *Top left:* Austrian Maria Theresa silver thaler (first minted 1780). *Top right:* silver riyal of the Kingdom of the Hijaz and Najd and Its Dependencies (1346 AH/1926 AD). *Center:* 10-riyal "hajj receipt" (1373 AH/1953 AD). *Bottom:* Kingdom of Saudi Arabia 10-riyal note. Photos courtesy of David Long.

bank, which greatly facilitated foreign currency transactions during the hajj season. Because the scrip was not issued as legal tender and was fully backed by silver and gold, there was no local resistance to it, and it soon began to circulate throughout the country. By August 7, during the 1953 hajj season, SR (Saudi riyals) 23 million worth of hajj receipts had been issued, and by September 10, at the end of the season, only 30 percent of it had been redeemed. By 1955, when a rise in the price of silver resulted in Saudi riyals being smuggled out of the country, the hajj receipts had become accepted as the de facto currency throughout the kingdom. Beginning in June 1961, after SAMA's charter had been changed, it issued the first paper currency, in denominations of 1, 5, 10, 50, and 100 riyals. In 1964, the hajj receipts were withdrawn from circulation.

Paradoxically, during the mid- to late 1950s, the period when the first government social and economic infrastructure development projects were being formulated, the economy itself was in shambles. King Saud bin Abd al-Aziz, who succeeded his father in 1953, was simply not up to the task of overseeing the growing oil wealth. In 1958, he was forced to name his brother and heir apparent, Prince Faysal bin Abd al-Aziz, as prime minister. Faysal quickly set out to bring order to the economy. Among other things, he secured the appointment of Anwar Ali, a Pakistani, as governor of SAMA for six months, seconded from the International Monetary Fund. Through the efforts of Prince (later King) Faysal, Ali remained for 16 years, until his death in 1974, the longest secondment in the history of the IMF.

Under Anwar Ali and his Saudi successors, SAMA developed into a foremost financial institution. In the 1970s, for example, SAMA was prepared to deal with the myriad problems associated with the dramatic rise in oil revenues, which could have otherwise created a chaotic monetary and banking environment. Among other things, Ali and his successor, Abd al-Aziz al-Qurayshi, oversaw the Saudiazation of foreign banks, transferring a majority interest to local investors. Thus the First National City Bank's Saudi operation became the Saudi-American Bank; the British Bank of the Middle East became the Saudi-British Bank, and so on. Characteristic of Anwar Ali, he began with the Saudiazation of the National Bank of Pakistan (now the Al-Josiah Bank).

SAMA was also instrumental in the creation of specialized government-owned development banks, including the Saudi Arabian Agricultural Bank, the Saudi Industrial Development Fund, and the Saudi Credit

Bank, all of which give concessionary financing to Saudi nationals, and the Saudi International Bank, set up in London in 1975 to train Saudi nationals in international banking.

King Saud balked at becoming a figurehead, and in 1960 he again took the reins of power. After two years characterized by mismanagement and intrigue, Saud was compelled a second time to relinquish power, and in 1964 he was forced to abdicate in favor of his brother, Faysal.

FROM OIL STATE TO OIL GIANT

King Faysal, like his father, was a man of extraordinary vision. The princes and commoners he chose to hold senior government positions have never been analyzed collectively, but they were a remarkable group. Many are still in office or are just retiring, and their places are being filled by younger men who were for many years under their tutelage.

As modernization and secularization went hand in hand, creating a development strategy that would accomplish this goal was difficult. It was a mark of his political skills as well as his foresight that King Faysal succeeded so well, gently pushing his people toward modernization, but no farther or faster than they could tolerate. For example, to meet the criticism of religious leaders that the radio was an instrument of Satan, Faysal ensured that prime broadcast time on newly established Saudi radio was dedicated to reading the Quran and discussing religion.

The Role of the Public Sector

The sudden advent of great wealth created a totally new economic relationship between the governed and the government. Saudi Arabia quickly became a classic example of what western social scientists call a rentier state. In contrast to most states, where the government collects tax revenues that technically are to be used to provide public services to the citizens, a major task of government in the kingdom is to distribute state-accrued oil revenues in the form of goods, services, social infrastructure, and subsidies to the people in the most equitable way. As noted in chapter 4, by 2009 the petroleum sector accounted for roughly 75 percent of budget revenues, 45 percent of GDP, and 90 percent of export earnings.[6]

Equitable distribution of the wealth is a far more difficult task than it might seem at first glance, with social and political implications that directly affect the stability of the kingdom. Moreover, to the degree that it creates public economic dependence on the government funding—a classic symptom of the rentier state—and saps the private sector of initiative and industriousness, it could end up a very mixed blessing indeed.

There are two major avenues for distributing public wealth: granting contracts for development projects, and public and individual subsidies.

One of the major unintended consequences of oil wealth was Riyadh replacing Jiddah as the major financial center of the country, in large part because of government contracts. Government contracts do not automatically go to the lowest bidder, and domestic contracts to a great extent have continued to be negotiated on the basis of traditional business practices. Negotiating with foreign governments and multilateral corporations on economic development projects, however, changed more rapidly as the kingdom came to realize that traditional negotiating practices depending heavily on personal relationships and influence were often counterproductive.

Ironically, there is a certain egalitarian quality to Saudi government contracting practices, creating the opportunity for all income groups, not merely those at the top, to participate in the transfer of public funds to the private sector. Although western critics have focused on members of the royal family involved in such practices, in fact, the same rules are practiced at all levels of society. It would be immensely destabilizing if such practices were halted at the bottom while the most influential levels, particularly among the royal family, were still able to use their influence for financial gain.

Granting unofficial subsidies is another way in which traditional practices actually enhance stability. Much of the under-the-table moneys accruing to senior Saudi political leaders is not for private gain, but goes to ensure that government and military personnel have a stake in the regime and the motivation to remain in public service rather than take a more lucrative job in the private sector. These "extra-budgetary transactions" are more in the nature of maintaining high overhead costs to co-opt potential dissidents and retain badly needed expertise in government than of corruption in the western sense of the term.

In the long run, such practices must be curtailed to avoid political friction among a growing class of technocrats who demand that government and business advancement must be on merit. The transition must be a careful one, however, to avoid the disruptions of practices that are as old as the Middle East.

Economic Planning

In contrast to the evolution of political institutions, Saudi economic development was the result of a formal planning process. In 1968, the then deputy petroleum minister, Hisham Nazer, was made head of the Central Planning Organization (CPO), a dubious promotion since the CPO was then a fairly moribund institution. Nazer, by force of personality and drive, reinvigorated it, making it the principal planning vehicle in the Saudi government.

This was a considerable accomplishment given the fact that the various ministries all jealously guarded their bureaucratic turf—a severe threat to central planning, which requires interagency cooperation. Nazer's former boss, petroleum minister Zaki Yamani, was a particular rival, even though they were friends. In recognition of Nazer's success and the rising importance of central planning, the CPO was raised to a ministry in 1975.

The central planning process that the CPO, and later the planning ministry, created bore no resemblance to a Marxist central planning process. Saudi five-year plans could better be described as a combination of wish lists and statements of intent. They are not intended as detailed instructions for budgetary expenditures, nor should they be considered outside the context of the rather flexible Middle Eastern sense of time. Budget allocations and target dates should therefore be viewed impressionistically rather than literally. The plans, however, are fairly accurate indicators of the direction in which the Saudis believed they should be heading at five-year intervals and what lessons they believed were to be learned from the previous five years.

The CPO, working closely with the Stanford Research Institute, instituted the first Saudi five-year economic development plan in 1970. With a relatively modest initial budget of $9.2 billion, it contained three primary goals, all closely aligned to the development philosophy of King Faysal. They were to preserve the basic Islamic religious and social values of the country, to increase Saudi military defensive capability, and to prepare the country for diversification in the post-oil era.

Although no one knew it at the time, the first plan was to overlap with the enormous rise in oil revenues beginning with the energy crisis of 1973. As a result, the economy expanded at a dizzying pace—the gross domestic product (GDP) increased 112 percent between 1970 and 1975—and would have done so whether or not there had been a plan.

The second five-year plan (1975–80), with a proposed budget of $149 billion, made the first plan seem minuscule in comparison. Continuing along the same lines, it emphasized social and economic infrastructure and building up the agricultural and industrial sectors, particularly petrochemicals. In 1976, the state-owned Saudi Basic Industries Corporation (SABIC) was created.

The Saudis also embarked on building two major industrial centers, Yanbu on the Red Sea and Jubayl on the Gulf. This was one of the most ambitious development projects ever attempted. The cities were originally designed to house a range of refining and petrochemical manufacturing operations plus a steel manufacturing capability, fired in large part by excess Saudi natural gas. The concessionary cost of gas helped the projects to succeed, but lowered Saudi Aramco's commitment to expanding domestic gas production, which may, in the long run, serve to dampen further expansion. In the meantime, industrial development at the two cities has attracted additional enterprises, both public and private, including fabrication and processing plants for both local markets and re-export.

The second plan also placed special emphasis on social welfare and development projects, including free medical service, subsidized housing, and free education. The Saudi educational system was greatly expanded, and thousands of young Saudis were sent abroad for further study until national universities could absorb them.

The emphasis on public education has continued. From a mere 33,000 in 1953, the Saudi student population rose to 2.65 million by 1989 and to almost 3 million in 2006. In 2006, around 700,000 high school graduates were enrolled in over 60 Saudi colleges and universities. In addition, thousands of Saudi students were enrolled abroad. This is a tremendous achievement considering that the kingdom was 95 percent illiterate at the end of World War II.

The second five-year plan coincided with the great oil boom of the 1970s and thus faced no financial constraints. By the end of the period, the lesson that foreign aid donors had learned in other developing countries had became obvious to the Saudis as well—that there are limits to how much capital expenditure an economy can absorb, particularly in the absence of an adequate pool of technical expertise, a bureaucratic tradition, and a well-ingrained work ethic. With a low absorptive capacity for capital expenditure, massive spending created inflation, waste, and graft on a grand scale.

Nevertheless, it was during this period that the Saudis succeeded in putting in place most of the basic economic and social infrastructure needed for a modern economy, created a viable non-oil industrial sector, particularly in import substitution items, and transformed the Saudi population into one of the most highly educated in the region. Moreover, they still spent considerably less than they earned in the 1970s, amassing foreign exchange holdings of around $150 billion.

When the third five-year plan (1980–85) was approved by the Council of Ministers in May 1980, no one yet knew that the oil boom was about to end and that a period of extended glut was approaching. The third plan had an approved budget of $250 billion, reflecting projected oil revenues that were wholly unrealistic in light of the greatly reduced oil prices that have persisted since that time. It was eventually scaled back to about $180 billion. Nevertheless, the planners did have a good grasp of the state of Saudi economic development.

The third plan emphasized consolidating previous economic gains and reducing inflation, a major problem during the second plan. Due to the drastic reduction in revenues in the 1980s, the problem of inflation solved itself. The plan also emphasized social and physical infrastructure completion and Saudiazation, particularly in reducing dependence on foreign labor.

When the oil glut began in the early 1980s and oil prices started their long decline, the Saudis made a calculated decision to maintain economic and social development and military spending levels by drawing down foreign exchange reserves. They counted on prices eventually rising to put an end to deficit financing.

No one foresaw that the glut would last so long and that the Saudi national deficit would expand as much as it did. Not even a fraction of the billions of dollars loaned to shore up Iraq in the Iran-Iraq war were ever repaid, and Operation Desert Storm cost the Saudis another $55 billion. In addition, the continuing post–Gulf war military threats of Iran and Iraq prompted a higher level of Saudi defense spending.

The fourth plan (1985–90) was scaled down in size to under $140 billion, and it emphasized economic efficiency and productivity as well as the importance of a strong private sector. The fifth plan (1990–95) was reduced even more, to just over $100 billion. Following along the general lines of previous plans, it sets modest targets for expansion of social services and economic infrastructure and continued support for non-oil sectors of the economy.

The sixth plan (1995–2000) and seventh plan (2000–2005) were also to be scaled down, and they continue to emphasize strengthening the private sector, including more privatization. The other major goals of the plans, announced in mid-1993, are better rationalization of government expenditures (apparently reflecting awareness of the need for more strategic planning), manpower training, and Saudiazation.

With oil prices again rising, the eighth plan was a major turning point. It was designed to be the first step in long-term objectives to be addressed over four five-year plans extending to 2025.

Emphases in the eighth plan include privatization and more support for the private sector, particularly small and medium enterprises, addressing the investment environment and incentives and encouraging more non-oil exports.

THE SAUDI PRIVATE SECTOR

The predominance of the government-owned oil sector has often caused the Saudi private sector to be overlooked. Yet it accounts for about 40 percent of the GDP. As has been noted, free market capitalism in Arabia is as old as recorded history. The advent of oil did not change that either in Saudi Arabia or in the other Arabian oil states. As noted above, all wealth is considered a gift of God's bounty. It is considered the government's responsibility to distribute the national wealth to the people. On the one hand, because all wealth is a gift from God to his people, it is up to individuals and extended families to acquire as much of God's bounty as possible within the limits of the law.

As a result, a uniquely Islamic-Arabian public-private sector partnership has emerged in which a major goal of Saudi social and economic development programs is to create a strong private sector.

A case in point is the evolution of credit institutions. Private commercial banking evolved beginning with foreign banks and later the establishment of Saudi-owned full-service banks, and the central bank, SAMA, was created in 1952. Following a government directive, by 1982 all foreign banks had merged with Saudi banks that maintained majority interest. Also in the 1980s, new banking regulations were introduced that created service charges rather than interest rates, which were prohibited by Shariʿa.

During this period, a revival of Islamic banking conforming to Shariʿa and designed to meet modern banking needs was pioneered in Egypt and has expanded worldwide. Creation of the Islamic Development Bank (IDB) in Jiddah in 1975 under Prince Muhammad Al Faysal was a major step in the spread of Islamic banking. Since its founding, IDB has played a major role in international financing in both Muslim and non-Muslim states.[7]

The hajj service industry provides an even broader though seldom mentioned case of public-private sector cooperation. To grasp the magnitude of the hajj, one only needs to consider that up to 3 million perform the hajj each year. And because Saudis are restricted from attending more than once every five years, to make room for foreign hajjis, most of those numbers are from abroad. Moreover, because the huge numbers are making hajj arrangements harder to accomplish, up to 8 million perform the *umrah* during the rest of the year, even though it does not meet the obligation to perform the hajj.

When King Abd al-Aziz annexed the Hijaz in 1926, he wisely did not nationalize the administration of the hajj, and the ancient guilds have remained in charge of making hajj foreign travel arrangements and living accommodations and guiding the hajjis through the rites and the visit to al-Madinah. At the same time, the government strictly regulates hajj charges and fees and provides health and sanitation, traffic safety, and security services as well as issuing special hajj visas and providing special protocol for VIP hajjis. (For public administration of the hajj, see chapter 6.)

In addition to the service industry, the retail market created by the hajj, which was the mainstay of the economy before oil, was in its commercial context analogous to the Christmas season in the United States, the cornerstone of U.S. retail sales. The rapid expansion of the numbers performing the umrah, however, has increased the magnitude of retail sales even further.

Then there is the transportation industry. The Hajj Ministry coordinates ground transportation through the General Cars Syndicate. Private transportation companies that qualify with a requisite number of cars and buses can join. In 2008, the 16 companies that make up the syndicate spent $213 million for 1,000 new buses and contracted with 66 hajj delegations to transport some 1.5 million hajjis in 18,700 buses.[8] As the same time, one of the biggest hajj trade recipients is state-owned. Saudi Arabian Airlines (Saudia) was created in 1949 mainly to accommodate hajj travel. It is now one of the largest air carriers in the world and owns the rights to half of the hajj charter flights from abroad. Although owned by the government, it has a substantial number of employees.

Aside from the mammoth Saudi Aramco, which is the largest integrated oil company in the world, most heavy industry companies are subsidiaries of SABIC and either are fired by or utilize oil by-products. For example, Saudi Arabian Fertilizer Company is 41 percent owned by SABIC, 10 percent owned by its employees, and 49 percent owned by Saudi stockholders. The government, however, has encouraged private light industry, particularly in export-reducing products such as assembling window and door frames. It also subsidized water resources for irrigated agriculture. The future of agriculture, however, will have to take into account the ancient, nonreplenishable aquifers that have been greatly drawn down. Fresh water resources have become increasingly reliant on desalination plants and recycling of city water in major metropolitan areas.

LOOKING TO THE FUTURE: THE IMPACT OF RAPID ECONOMIC DEVELOPMENT

In contrast to the evolution and modernization of Saudi society and government operations, the evolution of Saudi economic development has been more rapid, beginning as it did only after the government began to acquire significant oil revenues in the wake of World War II. In addition, it has been subjected to a far more rigorous planning process through the continuing five-year economic development plans.

Given the available mix of natural resources, huge oil and gas reserves, but a scarcity of fresh water, development has been reasonably well planned and managed. In the short run, the greatest challenge will be to manage reduced oil revenues resulting from the current global recession. Due to the cyclical nature of the oil market, the kingdom has experienced periods of deficit financing before including one that lasted from 1980 to 2003. At the time of writing, it is still too early to predict with any accuracy how long or how deep the current recession will be. It probably will involve managing the national budget, which is likely to include significant deficit financing in the current recession and is likely to be exacerbated to some degree by the political opposition to lowering the deficit through taxation.

The greatest long-term challenge for economic development is to diversify the economy as global dependence on fossil fuels begins to decline. The Saudis are already considering capital investment in nonfossil fuels and balancing that with increased oil productive capacity in anticipation that global productivity will begin to wane. Obviously, the Saudi petrochemicals industry can continue to use oil as feedstock, but making the transition extends beyond that.

An area of particular importance is Saudi human resources. The oil sector is capital-intensive, and originally most executive and technology positions were filled by expatriates. Over time, trained Saudis have taken over these positions. But with the population explosion due in large part to rapid advances in modern health care, Saudi Arabia now has more young people reaching working age than there are available jobs. Realizing that, the government has initiated a Saudiazation program to reduce the number of expatriate workers.

But the imbalance of those Saudis reaching working age and available jobs does not tell the whole story. There are many unskilled and some skilled jobs that many Saudis refuse to do. In addition, many young Saudi males whose financial needs are met by their families are not seriously looking for jobs.

A decline in the work ethic due to financial needs being met has also lowered the productivity of many young Saudis, making them less competitive with comparable foreign workers willing to work for lower wages. Thus despite government efforts, Saudiazation has not succeeded to the extent originally hoped. Expatriates and their families now number about 5 million. In the long run, the Saudi labor force will need to be more competitive not only to make Saudiazation succeed but also to be more competitive in a global economy.

The role of women in the workforce is of particular importance. Female university graduates are often more highly skilled and work-oriented than males, and they now outnumber male graduates. Although millennia-old social norms forbidding mixing with those of the opposite sex who are not members of the family have retarded employee opportunities for women, those joining the workforce have steadily increased. In February 2009, King Abdullah named Dr. Noura al-Fayez as deputy minister for girls' education, the highest position held by a woman in the government.

Advances in communications and transportation technology have broken down the barriers to meeting and conversing with members of the opposite sex in Saudi Arabia, but it will take time to readjust norms regarding women in the workplace. From a purely economic standpoint, however, present gender relations norms are a great waste of human resources and could make adaptation to economic change more difficult, particularly in the advent of a post-oil world in response to climate change and increasing domestic and global population growth.

In sum, the coming of oil has transformed Saudi Arabia from a preindustrial economy to a major oil economy virtually overnight, and the key has been evolutionary change. The challenge for the future is to prepare for the need to make even greater strides to keep up with an ever-evolving global economy.

The Saudi Political System

Saudi Arabia is a harsh land, and until the discovery of oil, mere physical survival was a struggle. The imperative of survival bred stern rules of behavior and swift punishment for nonconformity that are still tightly woven into the social and political fabric of the country. One of the characteristics—indeed, anomalies—of Saudi politics is a harsh political system administered with a relatively light touch. In part, the light touch is a result of the ancient Arabian institution of public participation in group decision making through consultation (*shura*) with elders in order to reach a consensus (*ijma'*), discussed more at length below.

THE SAUDI CONSTITUTIONAL AND LEGAL SYSTEMS

Constitutional Islamic Monarchy

The Saudi constitution is based strictly on Islamic law, which asserts that all creation is under the dominion of God and thus there is no separation of church and state. Thus religion and politics are fused together: *Al-Islam huwa din wa dawla* (Islam is religion and state at the same time).

The most recent reaffirmation of that concept is stated in Article 1 of the Basic Law of Government, issued by King Fahd in a royal decree on March 1, 1992, which states: "The Saudi Arabian Kingdom is a sovereign Arab Islamic state with Islam as its religion; God's book [the Quran] and the Sunna [the traditions, or inspired sayings of the prophet Muhammad and his companions] are its constitution; Arabic is its language; and Riyadh is its capital."

Saudi Arabia is overwhelmingly Islamic and has always been ruled under the Shari'a, or Islamic law. The Shari'a is supreme in Saudi Arabia, even over the king. As divine law, it is immutable and unchangeable.

As constitutional law, it cannot be amended. An often heard declaration in the West that because Saudi Arabia does not have a democratic system it is an absolute monarchy is not correct. Islamic law is supreme in Saudi Arabia, and the idea of the divine right of kings, used to justify absolute monarchies in Christian Europe, would be considered heresy. All litigation in the kingdom must be conducted in accordance with the Shari'a. No one, including the ruler, is above the law, and technically he can be sued for a breach of law in a special court known as the Diwan al-Mazalim (Board of Grievances).

In the context of government operations, the supremacy of the Shari'a as the constitutional law of the land rules out all statutory legislation whether by royal decree or by an independent legislative branch. What can be decreed are binding regulations as long as they are compatible with Islamic law and/or on which there is no mention in the law. This authority includes the king and ministries tasked with regulatory responsibilities, including the Ministries of Justice, Labor, and Commerce, the Council of Ministers, and the Consultative Council.

The Saudi Legal System

The Saudi legal system is based predominantly on Sunni interpretations of Islamic law, principally but not exclusively according to the Hanbali school of Islamic jurisprudence. As noted earlier, Hanbali law is the most conservative of all the Sunni schools, particularly in personal and family law. Thus many of the conservative social practices observed in Saudi Arabia, such as veiling of women in public, while not specifically required by the Shari'a, certainly have the backing of the religious establishment. On the other hand, Hanbali law is among the most liberal of the schools on commercial practices. To western eyes, commercial practices in the kingdom can appear far more free-wheeling than they are accustomed to. It would be a mistake, however, to assume that Saudis are totally without business ethics. As noted in chapter 5, the prevailing business ethic throughout the region is *caveat emptor* (buyer beware).

The Shari'a code of behavior is much broader than simply western legal codes of right and wrong or cultural norms of good and bad. As mentioned in chapter 3, there are five categories of human behavior, not just two. On the positive side are two categories: *wajib*, acts that are obligatory, and *mandub*, acts that are recommended and that bring rewards from God but are not mandatory. On the negative side are *haram*, acts that are prohibited, and *makruh*, acts that are reprehensible but not prohibited.

It is the middle category, *mubah*, however, that has provided the latitude for the Saudi legal system to address issues that have arisen as a result of rapid modernization. *Mubah* refers to those acts that are not specifically mentioned in the sources of the law and on which it is indifferent. All modern states must have some contemporary regulatory codes, and the Shari'a, developed 1,200 to 1,400 years ago, obviously does not directly address the legal issues of a modern technological world. Many Muslim countries have used mubah as a legal loophole for inserting entire western legal codes into their legal systems. Saudi Arabia has not done so. Nevertheless, there are many subjects that are legitimately mubah, and for them the kingdom has issued special regulatory measures called *nizam* (royal decrees). They cover areas of modern financial, commercial, and labor issues that in the West are subject to statuary laws such as commercial and labor contracts. In theory they are not legislated but promulgated in decrees, which are not part of the Shari'a itself but must be consistent with it. In addition, special administrative tribunals have been created to adjudicate labor and commercial disputes.

A major focus of Islamic jurisprudence is more on adjudicating disputes than on determining guilt, preferably before ever going to court. For adjudicating disputes between the government and private citizens, there is the Board of Grievances.

One other feature of the Saudi legal system not found in western systems is a binding legal opinion, called a *fatwa*. There is a separate Office of the Grand Mufti to issue these opinions. In contrast to American Common Law, in which there must be a case brought to court before a legal judgment can be rendered or an opinion given on constitutionality, a fatwa can be issued without a case being brought to the courts.

SAUDI POLITICAL DYNAMICS

Political Culture

Saudi political culture here refers to the impact of traditional Islamic cultural norms on Saudi political behavior. In a seminal article on the influence of traditional Islamic culture on politics, James Bill writes, "The traditional Islamic system has possessed remarkable resiliency and resistance to transformation. As a result, contemporary Islamic societies are the scene of particularly intense conflict between the forces of tradition and modernity. A deeper understanding of this struggle requires an examination of the forces and characteristics that infused these traditional systems with extraordinary elasticity."[1]

Despite the evolution of modern political reforms, Saudi political culture is still overwhelmingly Islamic and traditional. Islam is more than a religion; it is a totally self-contained cosmic system. The emphasis here is on cultural values, not religious piety. These norms have been particularly resilient in the face of change, despite the mammoth pace of modernization in the country.

As noted in chapter 3, a sense of inevitability and the compartmentalization and personalization of behavior affect interaction on every social level, including the political culture. One other cultural characteristic not directly associated with Islam is the high degree of Saudi ethnocentricity, due mainly to the country's historical isolation and geographical insularity. Arabia is the cradle of both Arabs and Islam, and Saudis tend to see themselves as the center of their universe. Personal status is conferred more by bloodlines than money or achievement, and nearly all Saudis claim a proud Arabian ancestry. Having never been under western colonial rule, Saudis have never developed a national inferiority complex or the other psychological baggage acquired by many colonized peoples. They not only see themselves as equals of the West but in fact believe their Islamic cultural values to be vastly superior to western secular values. Close personal relationships aside, they tend to look on outsiders in aggregate as people to be tolerated only as long as they have something to contribute.

Political Ideology

For the past 250 years, the teachings of Muhammad bin Abd al-Wahhab have constituted the political ideology of Saudi Arabia. Its main focus, uniting the Muslim community under the banner of tawhid, has served the regime and the people well through good times and bad. Indeed, one could argue that Abd al-Wahhab's Islamic revival is the ideological glue that has allowed the Saudi state to survive 250 years.

As political ideology, Wahhabism has not changed over time. It is and always has been a synthesis of traditional, unchangeable Islamic values used as a political response to constantly evolving social change under Al

Saud rule. What have changed are the expanding Saudi political environment and the increasingly polarized political reactions to rapid modernization and social change from both inside and outside the country.

Wahhabism has always generated a degree of hostility from abroad. Originally it came from Muslim countries whose political and economic interests were thought to be threatened by Muwahhidin military expansion. More recently, the hostility has come from western and Israeli critics who have charged that it is the ideological wellspring of all political violence in the name of Islam carried out by jihadist terrorist groups supported by the Saudi government. Ironically, the Saudi government itself has been the primary target of al-Qaida, currently the most notorious of such groups.

Even more ironically from an ideological standpoint, much of the justification for militant jihadism stems from the writings of Ibn Taymiyya, which were a major source of inspiration for Shaykh Muhammad bin Abd al-Wahhab. Ibn Taymiyya reinterpreted the concept of jahiliyya, "the age of ignorance," which in Islamic historiography refers to the period before Islam, claiming that the term applied not only to those who lived before Islam but to people still living who did not follow God's law. For militant jihadists, this expansion of the concept of jihad has been seen as a license to attack any and all perceived adversaries including fellow Muslims.

Wahhabism subscribes to the concept of jihad, including if necessary the use of force to defend the faith. And some more reactionary Saudi clerics have been quoted supporting violent political acts in the name of jihad. But the broader meaning of jihad extends far beyond holy war. It is the obligation to encourage virtue and resist evil in one's personal as well as community life. A Saudi friend once revealed that in the 1980s a friend of his sought the advice of Shaykh Abd al-Aziz bin Baz, one of the foremost and most conservative Saudi Islamic scholars of his time. He asked the shaykh whether he should make his jihad fighting the communists in Afghanistan. The shaykh said no, his parents were old and needed him, and he should make his [personal] jihad at home.[2]

That is not to imply that militant, fundamentalist Salafi ideology has not been a problem in Saudi Arabia. Since the end of the cold war and the return of Saudi fighters against the Soviets in Afghanistan, there has been a rise in militant young Saudis joining terrorist groups. Their underlying motive, however, is not to encourage virtue and oppose evil. It is to seek an outlet for all the pent-up hostility caused mainly by the fears, grievances, frustration, and rage that accompany rapid social change and modernization. More to the point, while some adherents of the Wahhabi reform movement have indeed become militant jihadists, the numbers certainly have never included all or even most followers of Wahhabism as a religious reform movement. By the same token, few jihadists are Wahhabis. The teachings of the late Egyptian Islamist militant Sayyid Qutb, who was also influenced by Ibn Taymiyya, have had a far greater influence on modern jihadists, including Osama bin Laden, than have the teachings of Ibn Abd al-Wahhab. Bin Laden's al-Qaida preaches jihad, but Abd al-Wahhab's reform movement preaches tawhid.

The Saudi Decision-Making Process

Because nearly all major policy issues are viewed from multiple contexts, it would be a mistake always to seek an overarching rationale in Saudi decision making. Saudi politics operate on many levels: Islamic world politics, Arab world politics, Saudi state politics, Saudi regional interests (Najdis from central Arabia tend to dominate the political system), tribal and extended family loyalties and obligations, and considerations of personal ambition. Probably the strongest loyalty is to the extended family, and no major political decision is ever totally devoid of considerations about how it will affect the ruling Al Saud family's welfare and survivability.

The Saudi political decision-making process often appears arbitrary and capricious to the casual observer, but it does contain a systemic logic. The creation of formal institutions over the past 60 years has made government operations a great deal more orderly but has not fundamentally changed the informal process at the heart of the system. This process incorporates two fundamental concepts: *ijma'* (consensus) and *shura* (consultation). Consensus has been used to legitimize all group decisions in the Arab world for millennia and has even been incorporated into Islam. The consensus of the Muslim community on a matter of interpretation of the Shari'a is considered authoritative. Even a Saudi king, despite all the powers concentrated in him, cannot act without consensus. With a consensus, the government can move with astonishing speed; without it, years can go by with no decision made. Thus one of the chief tasks of the king (and, by extension, all subordinate Saudi decision makers) is to create a consensus for action and then to implement it. The king is both chief consensus maker and chief executive.

In order to create a consensus of support, a leader must engage in consultation (shura) with those deemed most competent, influential, and personally loyal to him. Shura is a two-way street, with the person consulted actively participating in the decision-making process. Arabic has another word for consultation, *tashawur*, which means merely soliciting an opinion. This type of consultation also takes place in Saudi Arabia, but it does not constitute participation in the political process.

In the oil age, the traditional consultation/consensus decision-making process is under heavy pressure. Government operations are too large and complicated for an informal, personalized process always to work effectively or fairly. As a result, decisions are becoming more capricious. Even when a leader seeks to engage in shura, he can end up with tashawur, rationalizing that the people who were consulted were participating in the process. Still, for sustained increase in public participation in the decision-making process, it is necessary for the process to incorporate some form of the consultation-consensus process.

A major implication of the personalization of behavior on Saudi politics is the influence of personal relationships on decision making. It is not enough to know the bureaucratic chain of command in seeking to understand how decisions are made. One must also know who can exert personal influence and on what range of decisions.

SAUDI POLITICAL INSTITUTIONS

The Hijaz and the Early Evolution of Saudi Political Institutions

Other than the formal Islamic legal system administered by the religious establishment and the informal, unwritten tribal law governing the behavior of large tribal groups, Najd, originally an amirate and upgraded by Abd al-Aziz to a sultanate, had almost no formal political institutions. Abd al-Aziz Ibn Saud ruled Najd in a highly personalized way through shura with leading members of the royal family, tribal and religious leaders, and an entourage of confidants and advisors, all of whom were members of the royal diwan (court). It is interesting to note that one of his most trusted advisors was his sister, Nura.

It was the annexation of the Hijaz in 1926 that the evolution from personalized rule to rule through bureaucratic political institutions began. In part, Abd al-Aziz left the Hijazi political institutions intact to reassure the local inhabitants and the Muslim world in general that rule of law in the Muslim holy places would prevail and that the safety of the persons and properties of all pilgrims would be protected.

But the king also recognized that the Hijaz had a much more formal and sophisticated system of government, including cabinet ministers, and he also had the vision to realize the value of integrating those institutions into his existing governmental system.

The early development of Saudi national political institutions, therefore, can be seen as a process by which more advanced Hijazi institutions, with little planning, were slowly adapted to the political and bureaucratic needs of the country as a whole. As national institutions were created, their counterpart Hijazi institutions were gradually phased out. From a public administration viewpoint, it might have been considered inefficient. But given that it required commensurate cultural and political change as well, all of which took time, it was effective.

Paralleling the evolution of public administration was the evolution of public policy making from a totally personalized system run directly by the king to a more institutionalized system, still highly personalized but with a more bureaucratic structure and more standardized procedures.

On August 29, 1926, Abd al-Aziz promulgated a new constitution for the Hijaz, al-Ta'limat al-Asasiyya lil-Mamlaka al-Hijaziyya (Basic Instructions for the Kingdom of the Hijaz).[3] These instructions reaffirmed many of the political institutions already in existence in the Hijaz. Public administration was divided into six basic areas—foreign affairs, finance, interior affairs, education, Shari'a (judicial) affairs, and military affairs. In 1927 the first three were institutionalized into agencies, and in 1931 they were elevated to ministries. Most of the governmental machinery was handled by the interior agency, which included departments of public health, public instruction, posts and telegraphs, maritime health and quarantine, public security, Islamic courts, and municipalities. Executive powers were vested in a viceroy, King Abd al-Aziz's second surviving son, Faysal bin Abd al-Aziz.

The Basic Instructions also preserved the Hijazi Consultative Council (Majlis al-Shura), a quasi-legislative body whose members were appointed. In early 1927, Abd al-Aziz asked the ulama of Najd (ulama is the plural of 'alim, a recognized Islamic legal scholar) for a fatwa to approve expanding there and the rest of his realm. However, the fatwa concluded that the council was a legislative body, and Islamic law denied the right to make statutory law.[4] The Hijazi Majlis al-Shura was reorganized in 1928, presided over by the viceroy. Although it was never formally abolished, it fell into disuse and ceased to function in the mid-1930s.

The closest thing the Hijaz had to a formal cabinet was the Executive Council created in 1927 and chaired by the viceroy. It included ranking officials in foreign affairs and finance and the head of the Majlis al-Shura. In 1931, it was elevated to the Council of Deputies (Majlis al-Nawwab); and while it technically had jurisdiction only in the Hijaz, its scope of activities increasingly expanded to include the whole kingdom. A less-structured vice-regal diwan also was established and, like the royal diwan, functioned somewhat like an inner cabinet. Many important princes and other leaders maintained regular diwans as a means of providing direct access and consultation to the leadership for the people.

Retaining a separate set of Hijazi political institutions did not mean that King Abd al-Aziz administered the Hijaz and Najd as totally separate entities. As noted, the Hijazi Council of Deputies served the entire country. The same held true for public administration, which was still highly personalized. Thus if the king felt that a Hijazi ministry was the appropriate agency to perform some task in Najd or al-Hasa, it would be so tasked. Likewise, many of Prince Faysal's vice-regal decrees were applied throughout the country as if they were royal decrees.

From that beginning, Saudi political institutions have evolved into a multidimensional body that, aside from the king, includes national ministerial government, regional (provincial) government, and a number of independent public agencies.[5]

The Evolution of Saudi Ministerial Government

The first nationwide ministry was Foreign Affairs, established in 1930 and headed by Prince Faysal. Ironically, as viceroy of the Hijaz, Faysal was technically still the Hijazi foreign minister until the position was phased out. Except for a brief period when he retired to private life, Faysal was foreign minister until his death in 1975 and could well be called the father of modern Saudi foreign policy.

Of possibly more importance to the development of Saudi political institutions was the creation of the Ministry of Finance in 1932. Throughout the 1930s and 1940s, the drastic reduction in hajj receipts had forced the government to the verge of bankruptcy (see chapter 5). The kingdom was so poor that the finance minister, Abdullah Sulayman, could keep the government accounts in a large black ledger under his bed.

Nevertheless, the ministry undertook whatever government tasks the king thought necessary. In this capacity, it played a key role in the evolution of the ministerial government of what had become the Kingdom of Saudi Arabia. Initially it was responsible for most of the administrative machinery of the entire government (much as the Hijazi had been before it). Thus many of the subsequent national ministries began as departments under the Finance Ministry, some becoming independent agencies before being elevated to ministry level. In 1944 the Agency of Defense was raised to the Ministry of Defense (later Defense and Aviation).

By the 1950s, there were a sufficient number of ministries that King Abd al-Aziz created the Council of Ministers in 1953 (Majlis al-Wuzara'; *wuzara'* is plural for "minister," which is *wazir* in Arabic). Initially, however, the Council of Ministers seldom acted as a body; each ministry acted virtually independently of the others, and the council rarely acted as a body.

Then in 1992, King Fahd issued decrees expanding the consultative role of the Council of Ministers. Under the new decrees, the council was empowered collectively to approve loan contracts (backed by royal decree) as well as the national budget, international treaties, and concessions.

To reduce conflict of interest, ministers can hold no other public or private positions and are forbidden to buy, sell, or loan government property. They (and other senior officials) can also serve no more than four years unless extended by the king. Invoking this provision in August 1995, Fahd named 15 new ministers and reshuffled 3 others after replacing 100 of 250 senior officials the previous month. The moves were generally interpreted as a means of acquiring and promoting deserving younger men.

In 2009, King Abdullah initiated another major cabinet and government transformation. He accepted the resignation of powerful conservative figures (the minister of justice, the chairman of the supreme judicial council, and the head of the public morality committee) and appointed the first female minister (deputy education minister). The move is seen as another step toward gradual political change, albeit always conforming to the general social contract of government and population.

Table 6.1. Members of the Council of Ministers, 2009

Ministry	Created	Minister
Prime Minister		King Abdullah bin Abd al-Aziz
1st Deputy Prime Minister		Prince Sultan bin Abd al-Aziz
2nd Deputy Prime Minister		Prince Naif bin Abd al-Aziz
Ministry of Foreign Affairs	1930	Prince Saud Al Faysal
Ministry for Finance	1932	Ibrahim bin Abd al-Aziz al-Assaf
Ministry for Defense and Aviation	1944	Prince Sultan bin Abd al-Aziz
Ministry of the Interior	1951	Prince Naif bin Abd al-Aziz
Ministry for Health	1951	Abdullah Al-Rabea
Ministry of Agriculture	1953	Fahd bin Abdulrahman Balghanaim
Ministry for Education	1953	Prince Faysal bin Abdullah bin Muhammad Al Saud
Ministry of Communication and Information Technology (formerly for Post, Telegraphs, and Telephones)	1953	Muhammad bin Jamil Mulla
Ministry of Transport	1953	Jubarah bin Aid al-Suraisari
Ministry for Commerce and Industry	1954	Abdullah bin Ahmad Zainal Alireza
Ministry of Petroleum and Mineral Resources	1960	Ali bin Ibrahim al-Naimi
Ministry for Islamic Affairs, Endowments, Call, and Guidance	1962	Sheikh Salih bin Abd al-Aziz Al al-Shaykh
Ministry of Labor	1962	Ghazi bin Abd al-Rahman al-Qusaibi
Ministry for Culture and Information	1963	Abd al-Aziz Al-Khoja
Ministry of Justice	1970	Muhammad bin Abd al-Karim Al-Issa
Ministry of Municipal and Rural Affairs	1975	Prince Mut'ib bin Abd al-Aziz
Ministry for Higher Education	1975	Khalid al-Anqari
Ministry of National Economy and Planning	1975	Khalid bin Muhammad al-Qusaibi
Ministry of Pilgrimage	1993	Fuad bin Abd al-Salam al-Farisi
Ministry for Civil Service	1999	Muhammad bin Ali al-Fayiz
Ministry for Water and Electricity	2003	Abdullah al-Husain
Ministry of Social Affairs	2004	Yusuf bin Ahmad al-Uthaimin

Saudi Regional or Provincial Government

There are currently 13 regional provinces, or amirates. With some exceptions, Saudi provincial governors, or amirs, have historically been members of the royal family, and all are currently members of the Al Saud.[6] As of late 2008, amirs of the major provinces included Salman bin Abd al-Aziz in Riyadh, Khalid Al Faysal in Makkah, Abd al-Aziz bin Majid in al-Madinah, Muhammad bin Fahd in the Eastern Province, Faisal bin Bandar in Qasim, Saud bin Abd al-Muhsin in Hail, and Faysal bin Khalid in Asir.

Throughout the twentieth century, the amirs had enormous power within their provinces, or amirates. For example, Saud bin Jaluwi, a member of a collateral branch of the Al Saud, and his son, Abd al-Muhsin bin Jaluwi, who succeeded him, made the Eastern Province virtually their own personal political domain. Modernization and the increasing complexity of government, however, have turned the position into more of an administrative responsibility than a political fiefdom.

Nevertheless, public administration at the regional level continues to be a source of considerable confusion. Most national ministries have officials in the regional provinces who report directly to Riyadh, but they must also work closely under the regional amirs.

The Regions Statute, issued by royal decree on March 1, 1992, does not greatly clarify the situation. Article 6 states that each regional amir must "supervise the organs of state and his employees in the region . . . , taking into account the ties of the employees of ministries and agencies with their competent authorities."[7]

Each amir must also have "direct contact" with the relevant national ministers and agency heads and keep the minister of interior informed. Although the interior minister is directly in charge of regional and local government, the decree confers the equal rank of minister on the regional amirs. According to the decree, each amir will be responsible for subregional governorates, districts, and local government centers. The decree also stipulated 10-man advisory councils for the regions, paralleling the nationwide Majlis al-Shura. In sum, a high degree of interpersonal rapport and cooperation is required between provincial and ministerial officials.

The Saudi Majlis al-Shura

The most recent major political institution to be created is the new Saudi Majlis al-Shura (Consultative Council) decreed by the late King Fahd on March 1, 1992. In some respects, its creation completed the process of expanding Hijazi political institutions to the entire country. For years, there had been discussion of reviving the old Hijazi Majlis al-Shura, but no action had been taken. One of King Fahd's first stated priorities when he became king in 1982 was to create a new nationwide majlis, but it was 10 more years before the idea was given substance. Some attributed the long delay to reluctance on the part of the regime. In fact, it was the Ulama more than the regime that delayed in determining what the new majlis's responsibilities were to be. Harking back to the 1927 fatwa, many argued that any institution that created statutory law was contrary to the Shariʿa, which is considered a wholly self-contained system of revealed law.

A number of outside observers assessed the Saudi Majlis al-Shura as an embryonic parliament and a possible precursor to democratic representative government. Whether or not it will evolve into a democratic institution, it should be obvious to the reader by now that as long as the Saudi constitution is based on Islamic law, it will never become a statutory legislature.

King Fahd undoubtedly saw the need to expand public participation in the political process, but in doing so he drew on the formal Islamic concept of shura to institutionalize what had been the informal means of political participation all along—consulting "people of knowledge and expertise and specialists" to come up with a consensus to legitimize public policy. It was apparent that with rapid modernization funded by oil revenues, the traditional informal process was no longer adequate to create a true consensus.

The majlis's purview is to recommend new regulatory decrees and evaluate foreign and domestic policies. Council members are to serve four years and meet in closed session at least once every two weeks. Every member has the right to express his views on any subject referred to one of the majlis's committees and to propose new regulations to amend existing ones without prior submission to the king. The agenda will be determined by the majlis president, deputy president, and committee chairmen.

Originally consisting of 60 members, the majlis was expanded to 90 members in 1997 and 150 in 2005. It was first convened in 1993. Among the appointed members have been businessmen, technocrats, diplomats, journalists, Islamic scholars, and professional soldiers, representing all regions of the country.

Breaking with tradition, most original members were young by Saudi standards, all in their forties and fifties. Thus, although most of them came from well-known families, it set a precedent not to appoint only family patriarchs. Many had doctorates from the United States, Europe, and the Middle East. Similarly, the Islamic scholars were young men with outside exposure, not the older generation of leaders of the Ulama. Junior members of the Al al-Shaykh have also been appointed, as well as a few from the Al Saud. The current chairman of the council is Shaykh Abdullah bin Muhammad Al al-Shaykh, the former minister of justice.

There is speculation that in the near future some members might be elected. In the meantime, the Majlis al-Shura has evolved from a purely advisory role to a partner in government decision making. Taken together, the main impact of the Majlis al-Shura and the enlarged mandate for the Council of Ministers has been the advancement of formal institutionalization of a very old Islamic process. It is a two-way process wherein those men consulted are active participants in creating a consensus that legitimizes government policy decisions.

The real test for both councils, therefore, will be the degree to which their members actually participate in the decision-making process (shura) rather than act as sounding boards or rubber stamps for government policies (tashawur). However they evolve, the adaptation of a classical Islamic concept to increase public participation in the political process reflects remarkable vision and creativity by its creators.

The Judiciary

The standard western model of government is three branches—executive, legislative, and judiciary—which in a democratic political system are separated and independent. That does not work in looking at the structure of Saudi government. Not only is the Consultative Council not a legislative branch, but the Ministry of Justice, located in the executive branch, constitutes the Saudi judicial branch.[8]

This does not mean that it is subordinate monarchial rule. Basic to the whole idea of Islamic law is that it is above the government. The Saudi judicial system is independent from government policy, and even the king is not considered to be above the law.

There is also a major philosophical difference between the Saudi system of justice and those in the West. Rather than seek to determine the guilty party, the emphasis is on adjudication of disputes without loss of face, a reflection of the dynamics of a tribal society where disputes can go on for generations. The system is believed to be working best when the case is resolved before ever going to court.

There have been a number of major institutional changes in the Saudi judiciary in modern times. Traditionally the head of the Saudi Islamic legal system held the title "Grand Mufti and Chief Qadi." A *mufti* is one who issues fatwas, and a *qadi* is the judge in an Islamic (*quda*) court. To some degree, the creation of the Ministry of Justice in 1970 was just a change in nomenclature, for many of the same people remained in roughly the same positions. But it was also an attempt to modernize the bureaucratic machinery of the Islamic legal system without changing the substance.

The head of the judicial system had traditionally been a member of the Al al-Shaykh family, but King Faysal appointed as the first minister of justice a highly respected but forward-looking Islamic scholar, Shaykh Muhammad Harakan, a follower of the Maliki school. Upon his retirement, institutional transition to ministry status had been successfully made. The Al al-Shaykh still hold influential positions in the Saudi judiciary.

In 1993, the office of grand mufti was revived and conferred upon Shaykh Abd al-Aziz bin Baz, who was already head of the committee for fatwas. The reason behind the move was apparently to instill more bureaucratic discipline over the issuance of fatwas, but it is not certain what the relationship is between the grand mufti (a leading and very conservative Saudi religious scholar) and the minister of justice.

When Bin Baaz died in 1999, his deputy, Abd al-Aziz bin Abdallah Al al-Shaykh, was appointed grand mufti, which left the two highest religious positions (grand mufti and minister of justice) in the hands of the Al al-Shaykh. However, the appointment resulted in furthering reconciliation between mainstream religious and political elites in the kingdom. While upholding the traditional pact of legitimacy, the two judicial leaders spoke openly against terror in the name of Islam, suicide bombings, and the "jihad of al-Qaida."

The principal task of the Ministry of Justice is to administer the quda court system. This includes general, special, and appeals courts. Because there is no case law in Saudi Arabia, judges are bound only to Islamic law, not to the precedent of other rulings. The king acts as the final court of appeal and a source of pardon.

There are also administrative committees under the various ministries to adjudicate labor, commercial, and other disputes. In addition, there is the independent Diwan al-Mazalim (Board of Grievances), which mainly hears cases between the government and private citizens.

In order to meet the new social and economic needs of Saudi society and the requirements of a modern economy, a gradual but substantial legal reform was mandated between 2005 and 2007, the first in 30 years. By royal decree, the judicial system was amended to create specialized courts for commercial, domestic, criminal, and personal/family cases. As a new qualitative step, the role and independence of the Board of Grievances were boosted, and it answers now directly to the king. A Supreme Court was also established, replacing the Supreme Judicial Council as the highest tribunal for appellation.

THE SAUDI POLITICAL PROCESS

The Saudi political process basically operates on three levels: royal family politics, national politics, and bureaucratic politics. All are separate but interrelated.

Royal Family Politics

The Al Saud family is the main constituency of the monarchy, and without its support no one can become king or maintain power. Technically, this support is granted and withdrawn by an old Islamic institution that includes leading public members, *ahl al-hall wal-'aqd* (the people who bind and loosen). In addition to the royal family, they include religious leaders, technocrats, businessmen, and heads of important families. In reality, the royal family has always dominated the succession process. However, it also requires a fatwa to give it legality. The only legal stipulation is that to become a ruler, one must be physically, mentally, and morally qualified.

Saudi royal succession, based on traditional customs, was marked by intrigue and violence during its first 150 years, and some observers believe that it still constitutes a major threat to Saudi internal stability.[9] Beginning with the creation of Saudi Arabia by King Abd al-Aziz in 1932, however, efforts were made to make the succession process more orderly so as to preserve internal political stability while conforming to Islamic law. The following year, the king formally named his oldest surviving son, Saud, as heir apparent. He also made clear that his next oldest surviving son, Faysal, should succeed Saud, thus creating the tradition that succession should pass down among his sons.

In 1992, King Fahd issued a royal decree formalizing the succession process in a new Basic Law of Government. The Basic Law stipulated that the king would name his heir apparent and could also relieve him by royal decree, to avoid disruptive political infighting within the family in choosing a new ruler.

In December 2006 and after long deliberations and consultations, King Abdullah took a major step royal codifying the succession process by creating the Bayʿa (Allegiance) council ʿthrough which the royal family would appoint a successor following the death or incapacitation of the monarch. In October 2007, the king issued bylaws, and in December a commission was formed consisting of senior sons and grandsons of Abd al-Aziz.

Naming an heir apparent must be based on the prior consensus of the royal family. But if no consensus were reached, royal family politicking could undermine the political stability. Thus in establishing the Allegiance Commission, the king has addressed the royal family concerns for ensuring a smooth and rapid transition when succession passes to the grandsons of Abd al-Aziz.[10]

Royal family politics also revolves around *ijmaʿ* and *shura*, consultation and consensus. Yet little is known outside the family about how this process actually operates. The family is large (an estimated 3,000 to 10,000 princes) and has historically been rife with rivalries and contention. Nevertheless, it assiduously shuns publicity and always seeks to maintain an outward appearance of unanimity.

Generation, seniority of birth, and sibling ties play an important role in royal family politics, and indeed in all Saudi extended families, but they are not absolute. Capability also plays a role. Generation is a major factor and outweighs age where nephews are older than their uncles.

Seniority among brothers is also important, as it has been since ancient times.

As noted, royal succession is limited to descendents of the royal family, but there are also various collateral branches of the family descended from brothers or former rulers. Two of the leading collateral branches are the Saud al-Kabir branch, descended from an older brother of Abd al-Aziz's father, Abd al-Rahman, and the Ibn Jaluwi branch, descended from Abd al-Rahman's uncle, Jaluwi. The head of the Saud al-Kabir branch technically outranks all but the king in protocol because its founder was an elder brother of Abd al-Rahman, but that does not necessarily equate with political influence. Another collateral branch, the Thunayans, are descended from a brother of the founder of the dynasty; they lived for a century in Turkey. King Faysal's wife Iffat, who was also a political confidante, descended from this branch.

Finally, sons of the same mother tend to act collectively. After King Abdullah, who had no full brothers, the most influential male siblings in royal family politics are the six younger full brothers of the late King Fahd, called the Al Fahd or sometimes the "Sudayri Seven" after their mother, the late Hussa bint al-Sudayri. They include Princes Sultan, Abd al-Rahman, Naif, Turki, Salman, and Ahmad. The Al Faysal, sons of the late King Faysal, have also been active in public service, including Saud Al Faysal, the foreign minister, Khalid Al Faysal, the amir of Makkah province, and Turki Al Faysal, the former head of Saudi intelligence and ambassador to Great Britain and the United States.

In sum, the primary mission of the royal family is to serve as the main constituency of the monarchy; they must have its collective support to be appointed and to continue in power. Senior princes generally have more leverage in royal family politics than younger brothers or nephews. At the same time, junior members often seek the support of more senior brothers or uncles to support them. Thus Saudi extended family tradition tends to blur the lines between royal family politics and national politics.

National Politics

National political issues have always been decided to a great extent by personal interaction. Today, however, with the growing complexity of government policy making and the commensurate decline in the influence of personal retainers in the royal diwan, the consultation process is increasingly directed to those with professional and technical expertise. Moreover, with the rapid expansion of more formal governmental institutions and insistence on the appointment of technocrats in appropriate ministries, senior officials are increasingly consulted on the basis of their official responsibilities rather than simply their personal ties to the ruler.

Virtually all major policy decisions involve some configuration of technocrats and senior royal family members. As noted, the highest national security positions and major provincial governorships in the kingdom are held by royal family members. Most of them are younger brothers of the king. However, several next-generation princes (grandsons of Abd al-Aziz) and members of collateral branches also have positions of influence.

In recent years, increasing numbers of young western-educated royal family members, including those from collateral branches, have entered government. As they have risen in the ranks of the bureaucracy, they have created a new category, royal technocrats. It is still too soon, however, to tell how they will ultimately affect the national decision-making process, but so far the most successful have won respect on merit as much as on rank.

At the same time, the regime has always realized the need for technocrats and has made sure that government positions requiring professional expertise, both military and civilian, are filled with qualified people. Most of the ministries requiring a high order of professional, technical, and administrative expertise are held by such qualified people. The senior technocrats have considerable powers both as principal advisors to the king in their areas of responsibility and as operational decision makers. One should note, however, that the technocrats function as professionals in the policy-making process rather than as independent politicians.

One of the primary means of maintaining coherence in the national political arena is the budget process. Each ministry and independent agency must submit an annual budget and compete for funding. With overall spending reduced since the freewheeling days of the 1970s oil boom, the competition can be fierce. Spending priorities are based to some degree on long-term planning and short-term necessity, but the budget process is a free-for-all. At worst, it distorts true priorities, but at best, it provides competition that can help weed out marginal budget requests.

Bureaucratic Politics

It is difficult to assess the degree of centralization in the national political decision-making process. As the head of a government that is increasingly intruding into the lives of the citizens through its control of oil wealth, the king certainly wields more executive power than his predecessors. If there were an archetypal rentier state (a state whose economy is dominated by public sector income—in this case, oil income), Saudi Arabia could certainly qualify.

On the other hand, as the government has expanded rapidly over the years, the sheer size and complexity of government operations have made it impossible for the king to be personally involved in all of the pressing national issues requiring a decision. For lesser decisions, the locus of power is quite often at the ministerial or agency level. Because of a general tendency toward personalization of politics and because many of the ministries predate the founding of the Saudi Council of Ministers, there is often keen competition among them for resources and a great deal of overlapping responsibility.

All the ministries are highly independent, and bureaucratic infighting among them can be fierce. Although tasks are still assigned to officials for tasks beyond their bureaucratic purview due to personal preference, political influence, and force of habit, ministries and agencies jealously guard their prerogatives. For instance, they tend to have a proprietary attitude toward foreign companies contracted to perform services for them. It is seldom that a firm with a major contract with one ministry can be successful in bidding on a major contract with another ministry, particularly without the first ministry's tacit consent.

In general, the evolution of public administration in Saudi Arabia has consisted of a gradual shift to a more institutionalized, bureaucratized government. Bureaucratic procedures have become increasingly important in decision making and constitute a growing constraint on arbitrary and capricious policies. Personalized politics have been rechanneled from the traditional system to the present bureaucratic structure, and it is within that structure that bureaucratic politics have flourished in Saudi Arabia.

The creation of a government bureaucracy, however, has not greatly diminished the high degree of personalization in the decision-making process. Delegation of authority through an established chain of command is still very weak, and even the most trivial decisions are often made by a handful of men at senior levels.

With the expansion of government operations, the bureaucracy has also developed as an important means of participation in the political process. Senior technocrats can wield extraordinary power, at least in an operational sense. For many years, this acted as an important brake to rising demands for more political participation. With almost no room for expansion, however, and with many positions held by relatively young men who can reasonably be expected to remain in government for many years, access to political participation through the bureaucracy is increasingly being denied to younger Saudis.

In sum, the measured but steady expansion of public participation in the political process over the years has maintained a balance between the two poles of those who seek more rapid reform and those who would turn the clock to erase the stresses and fears created by rapid modernization. The recent moves by King Abdullah opening the way for more official and transparent participation of elected representatives, therefore, can be seen as a continuation of evolutionary political change.

THE PUBLIC ADMINISTRATION OF THE HAJJ

Roughly 3 million Muslims visit Makkah and al-Madinah while making the hajj or major pilgrimage each year, and millions more visit the holy cities while making the umrah or minor pilgrimage during the rest of the year. Those numbers alone would make it a major religious tourist attraction, but the hajj is far more than that. It is a holy obligation for all financially and physically able Muslims to make the hajj once, and one-fifth of the world's population is Muslim. In addition, the regime that administers the hajj ruled only a remote, preindustrial desert principality in the middle of Arabia less than a century ago.

It is difficult for someone not familiar with the hajj to grasp the magnitude of the administrative problems it creates.[11] Try to picture 2 million foreigners arriving in Jiddah by air, land, and sea. There they are processed by health, immigration, and customs officials, and those without ground transportation are bused to Makkah where the rites are to begin and where they are joined by 1 million pilgrims from other parts of Saudi Arabia and neighboring states.

Following those rites, they must travel about 20 kilometers out into the countryside, where all 3 million will be housed in a great tent city to await the sunset of the holiest day. After sunset, all 3 million begin the trek to another site, creating one of the world's greatest traffic jams. For the next three days they celebrate a major Islamic feast that includes sacrificing a sheep. They then return to Makkah for farewell rites ending the pilgrimage. Virtually all the foreign hajjis make the trip by bus or auto to al-Madinah before finally returning home either directly or on a special hajj flight out of Jiddah.

But that is not all. In addition to aviation and ground transportation logistics, there are huge communication problems. The foreign pilgrims speak about 70 languages; most are middle-aged or older, and many are illiterate. Imagine what happens if someone gets lost in a tent city and cannot find anyone who speaks his language. Everyone has to have identification papers. And if the hajj takes place in the summer (it falls on the ninth day of a lunar month), daytime temperatures can reach as high as 56 degrees C (130 degrees F). In addition, the law of averages alone dictates that hundreds will contract some illness or die of natural causes (compared to any normal city with a population of 3 million people), and for many pilgrims, death during the hajj would not be unwelcome.

The Evolution of Hajj Public Administration

Hajj administration has changed so much since Abd al-Aziz first took it over that how it was done then would be virtually unrecognizable to those engaged in it today. The most obvious change is the number of those attending. From hundreds of thousands it has grown to involve millions. As a result, Saudis are now limited to attending only once every five years in order to make room for those coming from abroad.

When Abd al-Aziz conquered the Hijaz in 1924, his two avowed aims for the hajj were to open it up for all Muslims and to reform its administration, which he felt was corrupt under the Hashimites. The hajj service industry under the Hashemites had been entirely laissez-faire commerce, and from the beginning, the Saudis have considered the hajj a religious obligation and have made a concerted effort to ensure that it is administered fairly and equitably. Throughout their guardianship of the Muslim holy places, the Saudis have strived to uphold their sanctity and accessibility to all Muslims.

At first, many Muslim countries feared that the zealous Wahhabis would allow only the strict Hanbali interpretation of the hajj rites. In an Islamic congress called by Abd al-Aziz during the 1926 hajj, however, delegates resolved that only the religious authorities of each school of Islamic jurisprudence had the right to adjudicate for their followers which specific rites to observe. This injunction also applied to Shi'as, and after an initial reluctance, Persia, which governed the largest number of Shi'as, became convinced that its hajjis would not be discriminated against.

At the same time, Abd al-Aziz realized that he did not have the resources to nationalize it, so he wisely left the guilds that administered it intact. Instead, he enforced tight regulation of the service industry, transforming it into what could be considered public service industries. The government even collects hajj service fees and then pays the guilds for the number of hajjis they serve, ensuring that hajjis were not overcharged.

After annexing the Hijaz, hajj receipts became the major source of government income. It was not until after World War II that it began to accrue large oil revenues. At the same time, the numbers making the annual hajj began to expand rapidly. In response, the Saudi government has spent far more on hajj infrastructure than the country has taken in from hajj fees. For example, beginning in 1955, the government has spent hundreds of billions of dollars upgrading and expanding the two holy mosques in Makkah and al-Madinah. The Haram Mosque in Makkah, the holiest site in Islam, now covers over 400,000 square meters (99 acres) and can accommodate 4 million hajjis during the hajj. The Prophets Mosque in al-Madinah is the second holiest site in Islam, and during the hajj it can accommodate 1 million hajjis. Today, studies are under way to explore further expansion of the hajj areas.

Transportation is another area that has greatly evolved. Historically, most hajjis from Egypt, the Fertile Crescent, Turkey, and Persia came overland by camel caravan. In 1908, the narrow-gauge Hijaz Railway, built with donations from all over the Muslim world, began service between Damascus and al-Madinah, but the line was destroyed during World War I.[12]

The camel caravans were grand affairs that took weeks or months to arrive. The two most famous set out each year from Egypt and Syria, replete with colorful banners and *mahmals* (ceremoniously decorated camel litters). The Egyptian caravan also bore the *kiswa*, the black-and-gold embroidered cloth that covers the Ka'aba and is replaced each year before the hajj. Under the Saudis, however, the mahmals were banned as not strictly in accordance with the Shari'a. The kiswa is now made in a factory in Makkah.

By the time the Al Saud first began to administer the hajj, most foreign hajjis came by sea, and Jiddah was the primary port of entry. Still later, air travel became the most popular means of travel, although the network of paved roads through the Middle East has revived overland travel.

In 1945, King Abd al-Aziz established Saudi Arabian Airlines (now Saudia), with the transport of hajjis as his primary motive. The airline, originally managed by Trans World Airlines, was incorporated in 1963 as a semiautonomous public corporation under the Directorate of Civil Aviation in the Ministry of Defense and Aviation. Since then, it has become one of the largest air carriers in the Middle East, and its familiar livery is seen in airports around the world. During the hajj season, Saudia charters hundreds of flights to transport hajjis to and from the entire Muslim world. Saudi Arabia has agreements with other Muslim states to share this considerable charter business.

As hajj air traffic increased, Saudi Arabia was required to construct one of the world's largest and most modern airports at Jiddah, still the principal port of entry for foreign hajjis. One of the hajj pavilions at the airport is the world's largest single-story structure under one roof. The airport, which took many years to build, now accommodates more take-offs and landings than any other airport in the world during the hajj season.

Likewise, internal hajj transportation has also evolved, greatly facilitated by the network of paved roads that now blanket the country. Ground transportation for pilgrims includes bus service by the Public Transportation Company (SAPTCO) and hajj transportation companies registered in the General Car Syndicate under the supervision of the Hajj Ministry.

The huge growth of both foreign and domestic hajj ground transportation, most notably the Nafra, when 3 million hajjis "rush" from Arafat to Mina after sunset prayers on Standing Day. The Saudis have built more than a dozen multilane highways to facilitate the Nafra and installed the latest traffic control technology, including closed-circuit television, to monitor traffic. Still, the job is Herculean. The combination of those riding and those preferring to walk has created traffic tie-ups that can last

Figure 6.1. Buses at the Hajj terminal, Jiddah Airport. Courtesy of David Long.

for hours. By comparison, think of 25 Super Bowl or World Cup soccer games getting out at the same time and same place and heading in the same direction.

Public health and sanitation procedures at the hajj evolved separately from other administrative procedures but are no less important. The first modern hajj health regulations were introduced in the nineteenth century by western powers concerned about the spread of cholera. Beginning about 1817, hajjis from Indonesia and India brought the disease to Makkah, where it was transmitted to hajjis from North Africa and from there to Europe and the Western Hemisphere. Cholera epidemics reached England in 1831 and the United States the following year.

In 1857, the first International Sanitary Conference was convened in Paris to seek ways to prevent the hajj from being a conduit for the spread of cholera. In 1892, the first of a series of international sanitary conventions regulating the health aspects of the hajj was signed in Venice. The Venice Convention and subsequent conventions placed a great deal of the responsibility on the countries of origin. In 1894, quarantine stations were established at al-Tur in the Sinai and Kamaran Island in the Red Sea.

In 1926, an international convention was signed that granted the responsibility for administering the health aspects of the hajj to the Paris Office of International Hygiene, one of the precursors of the World Health Organization. The Saudis, who had just come to power in the Hijaz, resented this international administration as an infringement of their sovereignty. They were in no position to protest, however, for they did not have the capability to take on the responsibility themselves. Finally, in 1957, the World Health Organization transferred full responsibility for health and sanitation at the hajj to the Saudi government.

It is an awesome responsibility. Preventive medical procedures such as requiring vaccination certificates must be observed to control the spread of contagious diseases among the roughly 2 million foreign hajjis. But at the same time health officials must be careful not to impose unreasonable restrictions on any Muslim to perform what is considered a God-given right and religious duty. The Saudi Health Ministry must also perform curative medical services, and it has established an elaborate infrastructure, including first aid stations, field hospitals, and mobile health units.

One of the greatest health hazards at the hajj is the advanced age of many of the hajjis combined with the heat of the desert climate to which all hajjis must be exposed for long periods. Huge crowds are also health risks, creating accidents that involve trampling and being run down by vehicles. One of the most accident-prone areas is the Maqam Ibrahim (Station of Ibrahim), where it is said he used to pray and where a stepping-stone is displayed that Ibrahim (Abraham) allegedly used when he built the Ka'aba. Accidents are also common along the road from the Plain of Arafat to Mina during the Nafra and the areas around the jamaras in Mina during the ritual stone throwing.

In recent years, steps have been taken to alleviate another health hazard arising from the ritual sacrifice of animals during the Feast of the Sacrifice (Id al-Adha). The Health Ministry, in cooperation with Makkah municipal authorities, now provides sanitary outdoor facilities for the estimated 1.5 million animals and enforces health standards during their transportation. The standards must satisfy not only modern sanitary requirements but also the Quranic requirement that each animal be without blemish.

Disposal of this enormous number of animals after the sacrifice was also a problem. In years past, to prevent spoilage in the hot sun, great pits were dug where meat not consumed immediately was buried. Today, much of the meat is saved for distribution to the poor and needy throughout the Muslim world, a task administered by the Use of Sacrificial Meat Project of the Islamic Development Bank. Hajjis may buy a voucher from the bank to participate in the project as their ritual sacrifice. In support of the project, the kingdom has built extensive slaughterhouse and cold-storage facilities near Mina, employing thousands of butchers and veterinarians.

In all, health administration has improved dramatically in the past 20 years, but complaints continue to be aired each year. Nevertheless, considering the extremely adverse environmental conditions—a desert climate where hajjis spend considerable periods outside, the advanced age of many hajjis, and the huge crowds—it is a tribute to the Saudi government that conditions are as good as they are.

As numbers have increased and political stability throughout the Muslim world has decreased, public safety and security has become one of the most important tasks in public administration of the hajj. The Saudis have always insisted that the hajj is a religious observance, and they have banned political activity. Nevertheless, attempts have been made over the years to use it as a political platform.

During the protracted confrontation between the Saudis and President Nasser in the 1960s, Egypt attempted to create incidents at the hajj and raise questions about the Saudis' fitness to administer it. Until the collapse of the Soviet Union, Soviet hajjis were also used to promote state policies. In 1979, fanatical followers of Juhayman al-Utaybi and the self-proclaimed Mahdi (redeemer) Muhammad al-Qahtani seized the Haram Mosque in Makkah demanding political, religious, and economic reform. With foreign technical support, they were killed or captured.

Throughout the 1980s, the Iranians made concerted efforts to disrupt the hajj in order to challenge Saudi guardianship of the holy places. The situation came to a head in 1987 when 400 hajjis were killed in violent demonstrations instigated by the Iranian government. The incident back-fired for Iran, however, as most of the Muslim world blamed Iran for the incident and for desecrating the hajj.[13]

As was the case with the seizure of the Haram Mosque, most of the Islamic world was appalled by Iran's desecration of the hajj. This wide-spread reaction has not only reinforced a broad consensus of the sanctity of the hajj but has probably lowered the probability of violent political acts by sophisticated jihadist groups in the future. Nevertheless, due to the risks, psychological as well as physical, of such an act, public security and safety will likely remain a high priority.

The kingdom has a huge responsibility providing hajj visas each year for all foreign hajjis. The Foreign Ministry must begin months in advance each year to work with the pilgrim guides for each country. It is also re-sponsible for looking after high-ranking officials and other VIPs who are making the pilgrimage.

Hajj Administrative Management

Administering the hajj is a Herculean task. It requires the cooperation and coordination of the Ministries of Hajj; Islamic Affairs, Endowments, Call and Guidance; Foreign Affairs; Interior; Finance; Culture and In-formation; Economy and Planning; Health; Transport; Communications and Information Technology; and Municipal and Rural Affairs as well as the amirs of Makkah and al-Madinah provinces. What is particularly noteworthy about the public administration of the hajj is that, despite an institutional culture in which government agencies tend to act inde-pendently and in which intragovernment cooperation and delegation of authority are often minimal, the government units have worked so well together and with the private hajj service industry.

About five months before each year's hajj, the Supreme Hajj Commit-tee, chaired by the interior minister and made up of ministers and gover-nors, begins working on a master plan. The committee is also responsible for reviewing field studies for facilitating hajj administration.

The Ministry of Hajj has the principal responsibility of implement-ing the plan and coordinating all those ministries and agencies that are assigned specific tasks. In addition, it has direct supervision over hajj housing, food markets and water, mosque upkeep, and local ground transportation.

Daniel van der Meulen, who was for many years the Dutch consul in Jiddah and responsible for Dutch East Indian hajjis, wrote in the 1950s that, as the Saudis made the hajj a comparatively easy, safe, and healthy undertaking, they would make it spiritually cheap as well.[14] The opposite seems to be the case. Muslims seeking to fulfill their obligations to God have come in ever-increasing numbers since World War II to what continues to be one of the greatest experiences of a lifetime.

SAUDI POLITICAL EVOLUTION: THE PAST IS PROLOGUE

The success of Saudi political evolution is not based on where it stands today but on how far it has come in such a short time. Its continued success will depend on its responses to the nature and pace of modernization and social and economic change. One thing is certain. There will continue to be rapid modernization and a need to adapt to the changes it is bound to bring.

Past political evolution has been successful not simply for the political adaptations that have occurred in the face of change. It has also been successful because of what has remained intact. Although the Saudi political process has evolved markedly, Saudi Arabia's basic Islamic norms and values have remained resilient to change. Those basic values and norms have made it possible for the social contract between the Al Saud regime and the people to survive 250 years. Instead of abandoning those values and norms, the regime has applied them in adapting politically in the modern world, thereby maintaining the social contract that stills binds the governors and governed together.

In today's world, the standard for good governance is a democratic political process. But no political process alone can guarantee good governance. Many dictatorships have adopted a democratic process with elected presidents and legislators and a technically independent judicial branch, but no freedom. The key to good governance is public participation, not process, and how a society participates is based to a great extent on its cultural and social norms and values.

In a western democratic political process with majority rule, there are winners and losers. For the process to succeed, it is absolutely necessary that the losers (the minority) accede to the wishes of the winners (the majority). But by the same token, it is necessary to protect the minority from tyranny of the majority. In modern, nonwestern societies, those conditions do not always exist.

Public participation in the traditional Saudi political process was exercised through shura leading to consensus, which legitimized political policy decisions. Traditional Saudi society was very egalitarian, and public participation in the political process was delegated to tribal and extended family elders. For its time and place, that was sufficient. The key to success, however, was not representation but consensus. With consensus, there were no winners or losers. Since then, the Saudi political process has evolved to meet the needs of modernization, but in doing so Saudi political opinion has polarized. In such a political environment, a precipitous adoption of a democratic process with winners and losers could result in political deadlock and worse.

In looking to the future, therefore, the challenge for the Saudi political leadership will be to maintain the measured evolution of public participation in the political process while at the same time avoiding political polarization by following dictum of the kingdom's founding fathers: modernization without secularization.

7

Saudi Foreign and National Security Policies

THE SAUDI WORLDVIEW

As has been noted, Saudi policymaking is based on a combination of Islamic precepts and environmental conditioning that is quite remarkable. Foreign and national security policies are no exception. They are held together by a powerful perception of the world and the Saudis' place in it.

The Saudi perception of the world is influenced by an extraordinary cultural self-assurance and a heightened sense of insecurity based on being an insular people surrounded by enemies.[1] These two themes affect the Saudis' approach to international relations.

Saudi Cultural Self-Assurance

Saudi cultural self-assurance is based on two primary elements: a clear sense of Arab identity and a proprietary sense of its Islamic heritage. For most of the Arab world, Arab identity consists of a relatively modern renaissance or rediscovery of shared Arab linguistic, cultural, and religious heritage. It evolved from a political movement, Pan-Arabism, which began in reaction to European colonialism in the wake of the Napoleonic invasion of Egypt in 1799 and reached its apogee during the 1960s under the charismatic influence of Egypt's president, Gamel Abdel Nasser.

The Saudi sense of Arab identity is quite different from that of the rest of the Arab world. Traditional Arabian societies are largely tribal in origin, and bloodlines have always been the primary basis for self- and communal identity. Although they share a common language, culture, and religion with the rest of the Arab world, Arabians have never lost their sense of Arabian identity and consequently have never needed to rediscover it. Most Saudis, particularly Najdis, trace their ancestry back to the beginning of recorded history and their tribal genealogy even farther. The knowledge of their identity has given them a self-assurance that is unmatched in much of the rest of the Middle East. For example, identity crises, common among western-educated elites from traditional societies, are rare in Saudi Arabia.

The second source of Saudi self-assurance is its Islamic heritage. Common Islamic values and norms are shared throughout the Muslim community or "nation" (*ummah*), and thus all Muslim states including Saudi Arabia have the same communal Islamic heritage. A Pan-Islamic political movement in reaction to European nineteenth-century colonialism paralleled the Pan-Arabism movement but never achieved much traction. In any case, the Saudi view of its Islamic heritage is virtually unique. Most Saudis have a proprietary attitude toward Islam, a view that was substantially strengthened in the 1920s, when Abd al-Aziz occupied the Hijaz with the holy cities of Makkah and al-Madinah. As guardians of the two holiest sites in Islam, the Saudis have assumed an added responsibility as defenders of the Islamic way of life throughout the Muslim world. It is in this context that one must view the title adopted by King Fahd in 1986: Khadim al-Haramayn al-Sharifayn, or Custodian of the Two Holy Places.

The Saudi worldview, however, does conform closely to the classical Islamic view of basically a bipolar world composed of Dar al-Islam, or the territory under divine (Islamic) law, and Dar al-Harb, the territory of war—that is, outside the rule of God's law.[2] This worldview has been used by militant Islamists throughout the Muslim world, including Saudi Arabia, as justification for waging militant jihad against all perceived enemies of Islam. But Saudi Islamic foreign policy and national security policies, backed by strong public consensus, have always focused on preserving Islamic values and norms at home and throughout the Muslim world.

Saudi Encirclement Syndrome

A second major ingredient in the Saudi worldview is a highly developed "encirclement syndrome." Since ancient times, tribal warfare was a way of life; both tribes and sedentary principalities were constantly surrounded by enemies. From the Saudi perspective, those conditions still exist. Since

World War II, virtually every one of the kingdom's neighbors has at one time or another been considered an enemy: Hashemite Jordan and Iraq, whose royal families were forced into exile by King Abd al-Aziz; radical republican Iraq since the overthrow of the monarchy in 1958; Zionist Israel; republican Iran; the PLO when it sided with Iraq in the Kuwait war; Nasserist Egypt; the once pro-communist and now Islamist Sudan; communist Ethiopia under Mengistu; leftist Somalia under Siad Barre; Nasserist North Yemen in the 1960s; and Marxist South Yemen in the 1970s and 1980s. There have also been border disputes with Oman, Yemen, the United Arab Emirates, and Qatar and with Britain as protecting power in the lower Gulf, from their entry in the early nineteenth century until 1971.

As a result the long-standing Saudi encirclement syndrome has played a major role in evolution of modern Saudi foreign policy and the search for national security. At the same time, it stands in sharp contrast to the self-assurance bred of a strong sense of identity. The anomaly of these two seemingly incompatible themes existing side by side has created an ambivalence in Saudi foreign and national security policies that is not likely to change in the foreseeable future.

A word of caution should be added at this point. One should look with flexibility at the Saudi worldview. It is a perception, not a blueprint for policy action. Saudi Arabia is no different from any other country in viewing international relations in terms of its specific national interests, not as part of a rigid formula dictating a set response.

THE EVOLUTION OF SAUDI FOREIGN
AND NATIONAL SECURITY POLICIES

A century ago, Saudi foreign policy interests were virtually all driven by domestic national security considerations. At the end of World War I, for example, when Abd al-Aziz's son, Faysal, represented his father on an official visit to London, Abd al-Aziz's primary focus was on cementing good relations with Britain due to its hegemonic role in the Gulf. Even then, however, Abd al-Aziz was fearful lest western colonialism come to his country.

Today, national security is still a predominant area of Saudi foreign policy as well as domestic policy. But over the years, three other major areas of foreign policy have evolved: regional Middle East interests, Islamic world interests, and petroleum and other economic issues. It is important to note, however, that these four areas of policy interest are not mutually exclusive and that policy responses in each category can and often are incompatible with or overlap other policy responses.

Tribal Warfare: The End of an Era

The Arabian Peninsula was a violent place long before western technology brought modernized means of warfare. Vestiges of that violent world exist within living memory. A Saudi friend once recounted his grandmother's favorite story about a tribal incident before World War I. During a raid by a rival clan, she fled her family's tent carrying a box of gold coins. One of the raiders chased her for the coins, but as he reached for them, she picked up a stone, struck him a fatal blow, and escaped. Years later, my friend's story was confirmed by a member of the rival clan in another country whose uncle participated in the raid on the other side. The uncle said that the raiders had indeed seen her strike their clansman, but wrongly thinking he was trying to molest her, they believed he got what he deserved and did not give chase. It is hard to imagine such a raid taking place in the same century as the push-button Kuwait war of 1991.

The introduction of Wahhabism in the eighteenth century raised age-old tribal warfare to the level of a religious quest, enabling rulers to conquer and later retake large portions of the Arabian Peninsula, which they had twice lost in the nineteenth century.

Once he had united the country in the 1920s, Abd al-Aziz demobilized his tribal forces and had no standing army for almost two decades. However, many members of the Ikhwan, as his tribal army was called, were ill suited to the sedentary life he had offered them and rose in revolt. They were defeated in the battle of Sibilla, considered the last classical Bedouin battle, which broke the independent political power of the tribes forever. The king again resorted to tribal levies in 1934 for a brief campaign against Yemen led by his son, Faysal. Nevertheless, the kingdom had no standing army throughout World War II, although it clearly sided with the Allies.

In 1943, the king signed a lend-lease agreement with the United States to receive financial assistance, and the U.S. government advanced funds to keep the Saudi government afloat (see chapter 4). In 1945, Saudi Arabia formally declared war on Germany in 1945, but only did so in order to qualify for membership in the United Nations.

The Beginning of a New Saudi National Security Era

By the end of the war, Abd al-Aziz had embarked on creating a new national defense policy. He realized that he could no longer continue the luxury of not having a standing army, nor could he rely on tribal levies in an era of modern warfare. At the heart of the new policy, however, were the two major strategic goals of tribal warfare: to maintain a credible fighting force, and to seek a powerful outside ally against mutual adversaries. That national defense strategy continues to the present day.

In 1944, the king took the first steps to implement the new policy. He upgraded the Agency of Defense to ministry status, and he turned to the United States and Britain to help him create a modern defense force. In the process, he hoped to obtain a commitment from them to defend the kingdom.

The two countries agreed to send a joint military advisory mission to Saudi Arabia. But due to Anglo-American rivalries extant in the region at the time, they sent separate teams. The British subsequently established a training mission in 1947 to create a lightly mechanized force of 10,000

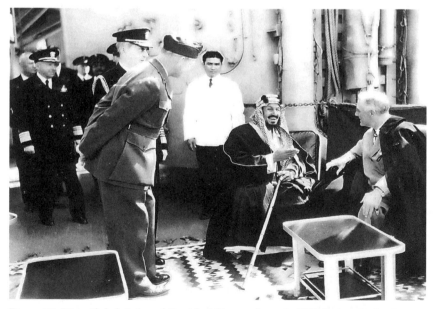

Figure 7.1. King Abd al-Aziz and President Roosevelt on the USS *Quincy* in the Great Bitter Lake, 1945. Used by permission of the Saudi Information Office, Washington, D.C.

men. Nevertheless, the Saudis increasingly looked to the United States for external security support, and in 1951 the British mission was phased out. From that time, the United States has been the primary, though not the exclusive, partner in the implementation of Saudi national security policies. Over the years, the Saudis have also accepted military training missions and security assistance from Britain, France, Egypt, and Pakistan and have purchased arms from many countries, including China.

Perhaps the first and certainly the most dramatic expression of Saudi Arabia's turning to the United States as its predominant western ally was the famous meeting between Abd al-Aziz and President Franklin D. Roosevelt aboard the USS *Quincy* in the Great Bitter Lake on February 14, 1945. The meeting cemented strong U.S.-Saudi cooperation in mutual security that has continued to be a preeminent mutual interest to the present day.[3]

The Development of Modern Saudi Armed Forces

The first U.S.-Saudi military cooperation agreement was signed in 1945. It provided for a U.S. air base at Dhahran, to be turned over to the kingdom three years after the end of the war. This changeover was to have occurred in March 1949, but with the advent of the cold war, a second agreement was signed the following June that enabled the Americans to remain at Dhahran until 1962.

As a part of the second agreement, a U.S. survey team traveled more than 44,000 miles in the kingdom in the fall of 1949 collecting basic strategic data. It recommended training and equipping a 28,000-man army and 15,000-man air force over five years. Although the recommendation, known as the 1380 Plan, was never formally adopted, it became the first comprehensive plan for building a modern Saudi military force. In 1951, a permanent U.S. Military Training Mission for Saudi Arabia (USMTM) was created, which has become the principal U.S. military training and development organization in the kingdom.[4]

In the wake of the partition of Palestine in 1948, Saudis were ambivalent about U.S. commitment to Saudi security, and for years the American embassy in Saudi Arabia kept a list of oral commitments to Saudi security made by every U.S. president since Franklin Roosevelt. For a country where one's word is his bond, those commitments were probably far more important to Saudi Arabia than most Americans realized.

Nevertheless, in the 1950s, Abd al-Aziz's son and successor, King Saud, flirted with Nasserism, apparently enamored with the charismatic vision of Egypt's president. Saud established a large Egyptian military training mission in the kingdom. Saudi relations with the United States grew stormier, leading eventually to the cancellation of U.S. base rights at Dhahran in 1962. Even then, however, Saud wanted USMTM to remain a sign of the U.S. commitment to defend Saudi Arabia.

The development of a trained Saudi army often seemed to move at an unduly slow pace. This was due in large part to Saudi ambivalence about a professional military force, an attitude reinforced by the number of Arab monarchies that had been overthrown and replaced by military dictatorships. Thus, while building up the military with one hand, the government sought to ensure against a military coup by limiting its capabilities. Reconstituting the tribally based Saudi Arabian National Guard in 1956 was seen in large part as a check against a military coup attempt. Another means of maintaining internal security in the armed forces was done by appointing commanders based more on their loyalty to the regime than on competence.

The slow pace was also due to the intense domestic political pressure in the United States, the kingdom's major arms supplier, to deny arms sales that would upgrade their capabilities. To some extent, however, the Saudis simply went elsewhere to purchase weapons.

As the need for professional competence grew, the Saudis resorted to more sophisticated methods to maintain security without impeding the capabilities of the armed forces. For example, they commissioned more royal princes, particularly into the air force, considered the glamorous branch of service, took steps to isolate troop units, prohibited combined force movements, and looked after the personal welfare of the officer corps in all or the service branches.

The Yemen civil war (1962–70) convinced King Faysal that the kingdom must become more committed to building a modern military force. In 1963, the Saudi Defense Ministry, working closely with USMTM, produced a second, more comprehensive plan. Known as Armed Forces Defense Plan No. 1, it became a blueprint for military development in the 1960s.

The plan failed to address Saudi air defense needs, however, prompting the United States to conduct a major air defense survey for the kingdom.

The survey was originally offered by Ambassador Ellsworth Bunker as an incentive to King Faysal to accept U.S. mediation between him and Nasser over the Yemen civil war. The king agreed, and although the mediation effort failed, he got his air defense survey. Completed in November 1963, it became the basis for the creation of a modern Saudi air force and air defense force.

In the mid-1960s, Prince Sultan, who had been appointed minister of defense and aviation by Faysal in 1962, began to consider a naval expansion program. The Saudi navy had been created in 1957 under the command of the army and still had no mission or organizational structure. In 1968–69, a U.S. survey team made a complete study of Saudi naval needs and recommended a small, two-flotilla navy—one based at Jiddah on the Red Sea and one at Jubayl on the Gulf, with headquarters in Riyadh. As a result, the Saudi Arabian Naval Expansion Plan came into being in 1972 under the direction of USMTM. It was, in fact, the beginning of a modern Saudi naval force.

In 1970, Prince Sultan requested a third comprehensive military development plan, which became known as the Leahy Report (named after U.S. Maj. Gen. Oswald Leahy, who conducted it). Although the Leahy Report, like its predecessors, was never formally adopted, it became the main development plan for the 1970s.

By then, however, unexpected oil wealth made cost no constraint, and Saudi military expansion increased geometrically. The size of the Saudi programs soon came under heavy criticism from members of the U.S. Congress, concerned primarily about the security of Israel. They argued that the United States was inciting an arms race in the Gulf. In fact, most of the expenditures were not for weapons at all but were devoted to military construction, including base housing and other facilities for personnel.

The principal rationale for heavy Saudi military capital expenditures was demographic. Saudi Arabia had a much smaller population than nearly all of its potential adversaries and covered a huge geographical area. Recognizing the kingdom's small manpower pool, the Leahy Report specifically recommended more sophisticated arms, which would create, in effect, a capital-intensive military force rather than a labor-intensive one. The air force received special attention as the only service branch that could physically defend all Saudi borders simultaneously.

This emphasis on sophisticated weapons systems continued in Saudi arms requests. Military purchases in the 1970s exceeded the armed forces' ability to absorb them, but the general principle was no less valid. Spending declined in the 1980s, but as a result of Desert Storm, perhaps the most technologically proficient conventional war to date, the Saudis saw the need to modernize their armed forces further. They therefore placed large orders for additional equipment. From the United States alone they ordered more F-15s, Abrams M-1A2 main battle tanks, Patriot antimissile missiles, Apache helicopters, and an integrated air-defense system known as Peace Shield. In 1981, the Saudis purchased electronic early-warning E-3 AWACS (Airborne Warning and Communications System) aircraft from the United States despite strong opposition from the Israel lobby and members of Congress.

Saudi arms purchases declined in the 1980s for economic as well as strategic reasons as the global oil glut continued to keep Saudi revenues low (see chapters 4 and 5). Nevertheless, the steady upgrade of Saudi conventional capabilities continued apace. During the Iran-Iraq war (1980–88), which was waged only minutes of flying time away from the kingdom, Saudi air force pilots flew defensive patrols over the Gulf along a perimeter known as the Fahd line and were able to scramble moments after being alerted of intruders coming close to the line.

The apogee of Saudi conventional military preparedness could be said to have occurred in 1991 when the Saudis participated in a substantive way in Operation Desert Storm to oust Iraq from Kuwait. They acquitted themselves well, for which the country took pride. That and the fact that the cold war had ended with the collapse of the Soviet Union appeared to have greatly decreased national security threats to the kingdom.

If viewed over a 40-year period, therefore, Saudi military development has followed a relatively orderly, consistent process based on a consensus between foreign military advisors and Saudi political and military leaders on how best to meet the defense and security needs of the country.

The Saudi Internal Security Services

Paralleling the development of a modern military force were the reconstitution of a tribally based paramilitary force as the country's major internal security force, and the evolution of the Ministry of Interior, which was created in 1951.

As noted above, the Saudi Arabian National Guard (al-Haras al-Watani) was reconstituted in 1956 from remnants of the Ikhwan (Brethren). It is sometimes called the White Army because of the flowing white robes (*thawbs*) tribal troops traditionally wear. With recruitment based on loyalty to the royal family, its original mission was to counterbalance the regular armed forces in a period of rising secular Arab nationalism and revolution throughout the Middle East. It has since evolved into a modern paramilitary force whose mission is to counter major domestic security threats.

Under King Saud, the National Guard was originally administered by a succession of his sons, aided by a small staff. When Faysal took over as prime minister in 1962, he appointed his brother, now King Abdullah, as commander of the guard, a position he still holds. In 1963, Abdullah turned to the British to create an advisory training mission to modernize the guard. Ten years later, he replaced the British with Americans, who created the Saudi Arabian National Guard (SANG) program.

The Ministry of the Interior is in charge of public security and law enforcement, including the national police, border guard, and coast guard. The current minister (2009) is Prince Naif bin Abd al-Aziz. He is also a full brother of the defense minister, Prince Sultan, which has enhanced cooperation between the two ministries on national security issues.

The Rise of Asymmetrical Security Threats

With the emphasis on conventional military threats, there has been little focus on the political and national security implications of the social dislocations and marginalization brought about by rapid modernization. As noted in chapter 3, the fears and grievances resulting from dislocations and marginalization generated fear and hostility among young people. Through the 1980s, many of them found a violent outlet for their emotions by joining the *mujahidin* (irregular warriors waging jihad, or holy war) against the communist Soviets in Afghanistan.

Their participation was noteworthy for several reasons. First, the mujahidin engaged in unconventional or asymmetrical warfare. The strategic objective of asymmetrical warfare is not military but psychological, the battle for heart and minds. It is to intimidate one's adversaries and their political constituencies through the use of terrorist tactics in order to obtain political objectives in the name of national, ethnic, or sectarian causes. Over the past half century, asymmetrical warfare has been used effectively by terrorist organizations and insurgency movements against far more powerful conventional military forces throughout the world.

Second, when the Soviets finally withdrew from Afghanistan, many of the mujahidin were convinced that they alone had defeated a super-power. And third, the end of the cold war left many mujahidins not only from Saudi Arabia but from throughout the Muslim world with no more communist enemies to fight. As among the Saudi Ikhwan in the 1920s, many Saudi veterans were not prepared to return to a sedentary life. Re-turning home, they formed informal cadres of recruiters of disaffected and marginalized young people with a predisposition toward violence to continue holy war against newly perceived "enemies of Islam."

By the 1990s, the terrorism in the name of Islam had reached a level that needed only a catalyst to ignite jihadist terrorism into an interna-tional movement. The catalyst was Osama bin Laden, whose persona be-came synonymous with international terrorism. A member of a wealthy and highly respected Jiddah family, bin Laden had won a reputation or-ganizing and financing asymmetrical operations against the Soviets in Afghanistan, He was still a loyal Saudi citizen in 1990, and full of hubris at their defeat, he had offered his mujahidin troops to the kingdom to drive the Iraqis out of Kuwait without the aid of the West, whom he considered nonbelievers and anathema on sacred Saudi soil. When his offer was re-jected, and when it seemed that U.S. combat forces might be stationed indefinitely in the kingdom, his militant jihadism was turned on Saudi Arabia and the United States. As a result, the Saudi government revoked his citizenship, and he went into exile in 1994.

In fact, the first two major terrorist attacks in the kingdom were not orchestrated by bin Laden. On November 13, 1995, the offices of the U.S. training mission to the Saudi Arabian National Guard in Riyadh were bombed, killing 5 Americans and several third-country nationals and wounding nearly 60 people.[5] Two shadowy groups, the Tigers of the Gulf and the Islamic Movement for Change, claimed credit. On June 4, 1996, an even more devastating bomb attack on U.S. military housing in the Eastern Province city of al-Khobar killed 19 Americans. The terrorists were later identified as Saudi Shi'a Islamists.

Nevertheless, by the late 1990s, his terrorist organization, al-Qaida, had become the most active and lethal terrorist group in the region and international in scope. His main targets, however, remained the kingdom and the United States. In 1998, al-Qaida bombed the U.S. embassy in Nairobi. In response, President Clinton launched a bombing attack at bin Laden's headquarters, but he was absent at the time. In 2000, al-Qaida carried out a small boat suicide attack on the U.S. destroyer *Cole*, harbored at Aden, Yemen, in which 18 seamen were killed. The same year, a series of car bomb attacks occurred in various cities in Saudi Arabia.

Lack of bilateral Saudi-U.S. cooperation against terrorism was not the problem. Following the first two attacks, the two countries worked closely together. The problem was failure to foresee that asymmetrical conflicts were becoming the major security threats of the future, replacing conventional military threats by other nations and their military. Advanced technology, the availability of training, and the low cost and availability of financial support enabled small groups, larger organizations, and even individuals to challenge political targets of countries whose military forces were far superior.

Recognition of the global scope of the asymmetrical security threat culminated with the September 11, 2001, attack by al-Qaida on the New York Trade Towers and the Pentagon. It was seen on live television around the world, and the entire American public was traumatized. Not since the Japanese attack on Pearl Harbor had such a crisis occurred on U.S. soil. The attack resulted in a mutual crisis of confidence between Saudi Arabia and the United States. From the U.S. viewpoint, the crisis was not caused by the initial trauma so much as by the U.S. political events that followed. President Bush's response to attacks was to initiate his military "Global War on Terrorism." In order to gain public support for this aggressive policy, he exploited the nation's trauma by using fear tactics exaggerating the nature of the threat. The tactics won public support, but had the side effect of adding credence to the vitriolic anti-Saudi and anti-Muslim materials by ultraconservative supporters of the Bush administration that were spread by the media.

The combination of American vitriol, heard all over the world, and the U.S. military occupation of Iraq posed a conundrum for the Saudis. Both incited fear and rage throughout Saudi Arabia and the rest of the Arab world, increasing rather than decreasing regional instability and raising the level of asymmetrical threats to the kingdom. For Saudis, the United

States, with which they shared mutual security interests, had become a major catalyst of domestic and regional threats to those interests.

With the passage of time, the fears and anger have declined and bilateral relations have normalized. For example, King Abdullah has provided thousands of scholarships for Saudi students to attend American colleges and universities. But there still remains a huge culture gap between the two societies that has created at best only a sacrificial understanding of the other in many areas. Despite the resulting ambivalence on both sides, however, mutual interests have continued to outweigh mutual differences.

The domestic Saudi wakeup call occurred on May 12, 2003, when, following the U.S. occupation of Iraq, multiple suicide terrorist attacks attributed to al-Qaida were launched at housing compounds in Riyadh, killing not only Americans but Saudis as well. The Saudis responded with a policy that has been in part draconian, taking into consideration that gentleness would be considered weakness by the terrorists. They launched a broad-based counterterrorism campaign that included shootouts, massive arrests of suspected terrorists, and closer oversight to interdict private financial support of terrorist organizations.

But their counterterrorism policy has also been enlightened, showing more sensitivity to the psychological nature of asymmetrical warfare than most western countries. The Interior Ministry has created a unique program for recidivism of captured Saudi terrorists. Although hardened terrorists can rarely be reached, the program has been widely recognized for successfully rehabilitating young Saudi recruits.

From an operational perspective, a reasonable Saudi counterterrorism strategy has also been put into place, coordinating the efforts of the Ministries of Defense and Interior, the National Guard and Saudi General Intelligence. Asymmetrical warfare is a multifaceted threat, requiring military, law enforcement, and security elements. But, because it is international and psychological, aimed at hearts of both leaders and public constituents, it also requires diplomacy and both domestic and foreign public relations capabilities. Coordination of so many different agencies, personalities, and specialized tasks is one of the most difficult elements of counterterrorism policies and requires constant oversight coordination and cooperation.

In the aftermath of the 2003 attacks, Saudis also began to come to grips with the fact that a number of terror problems were inherited from an earlier time. For example, King Faysal brought in members of the fundamentalist Muslim Brotherhood to counter the influence of the charismatic leader of secular Arab nationalism, President Nasser. With the decline of Arab nationalism as a vehicle for expressing political dissent, the hard-line fundamentalism of the Brotherhood began to resonate with disaffected young Saudis. By the 1980s many Saudis joined the mujahidin in Afghanistan, and others who themselves would not engage in violence provided financial aid to not only the mujahidin in Afghanistan but other militant Islamists as well.

In addition to external terrorist organizations and their domestic recruits and supporters, the government and mainstream establishment in Saudi Arabia are further challenged by radical religious fanatics who both participate in politically motivated civil unrest and preach violent jihad to anyone predisposed to listen.

They constitute two types of internal religious opposition: radical Sunnis who contest the elites' legitimacy and ability to protect the country from westernization, and disaffected Shi'as who generally feel discriminated against in a Sunni-dominated kingdom.

The first group consists of Sunni scholars, clerics, and activists, who were influenced by the Muslim Brotherhood and started to agitate against the ruling elites. Radical preachers in local mosques called on young Saudis to do something more meaningful with their lives and join the jihad in Afghanistan and Iraq. Some went even further by including corrupt Arab regimes as targets for jihad actions. Al-Qaida is a product of their inflammatory rhetoric, and the government is working hard to crack down on those radicals, arresting and reeducating them. Support is provided by the highest religious authorities in the country, who also recognize that more needs to be done on the ideological front to cut the relationship between militants, the disillusioned youth, and religious extremists. Some steps, like the ongoing interfaith dialogue in Madrid and current direct communications with the Vatican, are considered positive signals by western observers, but might be counterproductive with the more radicalized Ulama.

The other group consists of Shi'a activists and agitators. After the Shi'a tensions in the late 1970s and early 1980s died down significantly, a new round of clashes between Shi'a activists and government forces broke out in 2003 and continue to flame up, especially during the hajj or Ashura.[6] King Abdullah, through the National Dialogue and his reform agenda, uses both force and concession to prevent any impact of the conflict on the oil industry, which is largely housed in the Eastern Province.

Today, a general consensus exists among Saudis, modernists, fundamentalists, royals, and members of the Ulama and traditional elements (tribes) alike who vehemently reject terror in the name of Islam through a variety of activities. When the government sponsored the first counterterrorism conference in Riyadh in February 2005, the highest-ranking religious leader publicly denounced terror attacks, and the population has quietly supported military action in their neighborhoods against the remaining terror cells.

SAUDI POLITICAL FOREIGN POLICY INTERESTS

Until the twentieth century, Saudi interests in the Arab world were limited to challenging the Ottoman Empire and Egypt, titularly under Ottoman rule, to gain or regain sovereignty over territories in the Arabian Peninsula. With virtually all the Arab states having gained independence after World War II, and with the rise of Arab nationalism as a regional political ideology, the Saudis pursued a special relationship with the Arab states. However, as radical Arab states, particularly Nasserist Egypt and Ba'thist Syria and Iraq, adopted more antiwestern, pro-Soviet foreign policies, turning to Moscow for arms and military assistance, Saudi relations with the radical Arab states became at best strained.

Without the psychological baggage of other Arab states subjugated by western colonialism, King Faysal did not see it as the greatest threat to the Arab world. Saudis share with other Arab and Muslim states the classical Islamic view of a bipolar world composed of Dar al-Islam, the territory under divine (Islamic) law, and Dar al-Harb, the territory of war—that is, outside the rule of God's law. But Faysal saw Soviet communism as a far greater political threat than colonialism. His fear was not of Soviet absolutist government but of the threat of communist atheistic doctrine as a threat to the entire Muslim world, and he relegated the Soviet Union to the status of Dar al-Harb. Saudi cooperation with the Christian West in combating the threat of atheistic communism to the Muslim world could also be made to conform to the Islamic classification of Dar al-Islam, for Islam recognizes the other great monotheistic religions as divinely inspired revelation. They are known as Ahl al-Kitab, or "People of the Book." Sura 2:62 of the Quran states, "Lo! Those who believe (in that which was revealed unto thee, Muhammad), and those who are Jews and Christians and Sabeans [Zoroastrians or Parsees]—whoever believeth in God and the Last Day and doeth right—surely their regard is with their Lord, and there shall be no fear come upon them, neither shall they grieve."

Superimposing the classical Islamic model and the bipolar world of the cold war in Saudi Arab world political interests was not an exact fit. For one thing, the Middle East arena in which it was focused involved Israel, a Zionist creation, and also Iran, which though Muslim was not Arab. Another major problem with the analogy is that, in classical Islam, other "Peoples of the Book" were under Islamic military and political protection, whereas in the twentieth and twenty-first centuries it has been the other way around. Nevertheless, it was close enough for King Faysal to articulate basic Saudi Middle East/Arab foreign policy principles in terms of classical Islamic political theory. Conceptually, he did not include the Christian West in the Dar al-Harb but did include Israel, taking pains to distinguish between Judaism, which is recognized by Islam, and Zionism, which he castigated as a secular, anti-Islamic political doctrine. Characteristically, Saudi opposition to Israel has been fueled as much by a religious issue as by secular political issues—the 1967 Israeli occupation of East Jerusalem and the Aqsa Mosque, the third holiest site in Sunni Islam after Makkah and al-Madinah.

With Egypt siding with the republicans during the Yemen civil war in the 1960s, Saudi-Egyptian relations collapsed entirely. Relations with Yemen itself have been more complex. While the Saudis supported the Yemeni monarchy in the civil war and allowed imam (ruler) exile in the kingdom, relations between the two countries, although periodically correct, have never been cordial. Underlying causes of ill feelings include sectarian differences between Sunni Saudi Arabia and the ruling Shi'a regimes in Yemen, territorial disputes dating back to the 1930s, and Yemen's deliberately siding with Iraq in the Kuwait war. In early 1995 the Saudis agreed to negotiate outstanding disputes over the Saudi-Yemeni border, and in 2000 they signed a final border treaty. Thus relations improved to a degree but are still not cordial.

Saudi Arabia's current main Middle East policy interest remains restoring and maintaining regional security, discussed above, and as a corollary, reestablishing and maintaining political stability throughout the region. The greatest current threats (2009) to regional stability from the

Saudi point of view are the Palestinian-Israel conflict, the political instability in Iraq in the wake of the U.S. occupation in 2003, the mutual animosity between Israel and Iran, particularly in light of Iran's threat to create nuclear weapons and its long-standing ambitions for political hegemony throughout the Gulf, and the regional jihadist terrorist threat, particularly by al-Qaida.

Among the greatest sore points in Saudi political relations with the United States is what the Saudis consider the injustice committed by the United States in engineering the partition of Palestine in 1948 despite an overwhelming Palestinian majority. King Faysal, who was foreign minister at the time, also saw it as a major act of dishonor by President Harry Truman in ignoring President Roosevelt's personal promise to his father not to take any action on Palestine before consulting with Abd al-Aziz and the Arabs in general. In Saudi culture, breaking a promise is unconscionable.

In Faysal's view, the breach of promise was repeated by President Richard Nixon when, just days after he had promised Faysal that the United States would be "evenhanded" in the 1973 Arab-Israeli war, he announced a $2.2 billion military aid package to Israel. That dishonor was one of the factors in his initiating the Arab oil embargo. The embargo caused a second major crisis in U.S.-Saudi relations, a defamation campaign against the kingdom led by the American supporters of Israel, who apparently feared the power of the "Saudi oil weapon" to undermine U.S. support for Israel. The third crisis was the U.S. smear attack on the kingdom in the wake of the September 11 terrorist attack.

Though supporting the Palestinians, the Saudis avoided becoming too deeply involved in the peace process during the height of the Nasser era. After the 1967 Arab-Israeli war, however, radical Arab nationalism declined. And as a result of the Arab oil embargo, Saudi Arabia emerged as a major oil power. Befitting their new status, the Saudis began to take a more active role in Arab affairs, including the Palestinian-Israel peace process.

The Saudis hoped that the 1970s peace process would be successful, but they were horrified with the Camp David Accords and the subsequent Egyptian peace treaty with Israel. They believed that President Anwar Sadat not only had broken Arab consensus but had been seduced into a separate peace with nothing more than vague promises of Palestinian autonomy.

In 1981, Prince Fahd, then heir apparent, submitted the Fahd Plan, which he hoped addressed Palestinian core issues and tacitly acceded to Israeli insistence on an Arab recognition of Israel and security guarantees by affirming the right of all states in the area to live in peace. The plan, accepted in a modified form at an Arab summit in Morocco the following year, was totally rejected by Israel on grounds that the tacit affirmation was no guarantee at all. It is doubtful, however, that had it been explicit, Israel would have been willing to address the Palestinian core issues, and without its doing so, there appears little chance of a negotiated settlement.

Nevertheless, the Saudis have continued to work for a peace settlement. From their viewpoint, the main obstacle remains Israel's intransigence in refusing to address core Palestinian issues for a two state settlement: borders based generally on UN Security Council Resolution 242, acceptance of a shared responsibility to adjudicate the Palestinian refugee problem, the illegal Jewish settlements in the Palestinian West Bank, and the political status of Jerusalem, which Sunni Muslims consider the third holiest city in Islam after Makkah and al-Madinah.

The Saudis had high hopes in 2000 that incoming president George W. Bush would finally make what they considered real progress toward an Arab-Israeli peace settlement. In the early months of his first administration, Bush shied away from Middle East politics, although in June 2001, he became the first U.S. president to state explicitly that the Palestinians should have an independent state. Bush's strong support of Israel caused the Saudis to continue seeking a settlement on their own. In 2002, Prince Abdullah submitted a comprehensive peace plan that was adopted by the Arab League. But as with previous peace initiatives, it went nowhere.

As king, Abdullah continues his efforts to bring unity to Palestinian political factions as a step toward a negotiated settlement, but without the political will of either the Palestinians or the Israelis to accede to the other's terms, there is not likely to be a settlement without outside pressure. The Saudis have hopes that President Barack Obama might be able to restart the peace process despite the election of the right-wing Israeli government in early 2009, but first Obama will have to create the domestic U.S. political will to do so in the face of Israeli objections.

The second greatest current regional threats facing the kingdom are the political instability resulting from the U.S. occupation of Iraq and the confrontational foreign policies of Iran. There is little the kingdom can do about Iraq except to wait and see what will happen after the American troops are pulled out. In a worse-case scenario, however, if protracted, large-scale ethnic and/or sectarian violence breaks out in Iraq once the United States withdraws, it could spread far beyond Iraq and threaten stability throughout the entire Gulf region.

Of all the Middle East states, Iran is perceived by the Saudis to pose the greatest potential security threat. From an ethnic perspective, Arab-Persian relations have never been cordial, not only in political terms but also in sectarian and cultural terms. An important element of Iranian identity is its ancient Persian civilization and imperial past. Whether or not Iran has any current plans to seek hegemony in the Gulf, it still has dreams of imperial glory. In sectarian terms, the regime in Iran is fiercely Shi'a, and many Saudi Sunnis believe that Shi'ism is heresy. Moreover, Iran has in the past tried to challenge Saudi Arabia for leadership of the Muslim world.

From an operational viewpoint, Saudis do not share Israeli paranoia that Iran is not only in the process of developing nuclear weapons but intends to use them against its adversaries. But Saudis are very concerned that Iranian nuclear capabilities could be used as nuclear blackmail in the Gulf in an attempt to gain political hegemony. In the meantime, Israeli fears of Iranian capabilities and intentions have increased the confrontational response of Iran and have added to overall political instability.

Furthermore, there are Saudi concerns that Iran might encourage and support terrorist or insurgent groups made up of disaffected young Saudi Shi'as and possibly even radicalized Sunnis in order to destabilize or even to threaten to destabilize the Saudi regime. Though frustrated over being second-class citizens in many ways, the Saudi Shi'as are Arabs and have not shown any interest in becoming second-class Shi'as under Tehran. Nevertheless, terrorism is small-group psychological activity, and it would not take a large number of dissidents to create an incident that attracts media coverage. The Saudi government has been sensitive to its Shi'a minority's frustrations, but it will be a continuing problem.

Commensurate with their historical use of diplomacy as well as force, the Saudis have for many years now sought to create an environment of mutual coexistence with Iran, often despite strong criticism from U.S. administrations. With the Obama administration now sharing the same view, it remains the best option for reducing tensions.

Saudi Islamic Foreign Policy Interests

From the time that King Abd al-Aziz annexed the Hijaz, he felt deeply the responsibility he had to the entire Muslim world as ruler of the cradle of Islam, keeper of the two holiest places and host to the annual hajj. As noted in chapter 6, this responsibility was originally focused on making the hajj accessible physically and financially to all Muslims by imposing oversight on the private hajj service industry and regulating its activities, including collection of fees. Since Saudi Arabia emerged as a major oil-producing state after World War II and attendance at the hajj began rapidly to expand, the government has spent billions of dollars on hajj infrastructure. Moreover, its administration of the hajj has expanded into a worldwide operation, providing special hajj visas for foreign hajjis and overseeing the global responsibilities of the service industry in providing for round-trip transportation.

By the time King Fahd institutionalized Saudi hajj responsibilities in 1986 by adopting the title Custodian of the Two Holy Places (Makkah and al-Madinah), the kingdom perceived that its role included acting in effect as the conscience for the entire Muslim world. One aspect of the expanded Saudi Islamic role has been providing food and financial aid to Muslim countries suffering from war or natural disasters. The program for preserving meat from animals sacrificed during the Id al-Adha at the end of the hajj and distributing it throughout the Muslim world is part of that policy.

The Saudi role in hosting the hajj was purely religious. Indeed, the kingdom would not allow it to become a political platform. As noted, however, King Faysal sought to revive Pan-Islamism as a political vehicle to challenge Nasser's secular Pan-Arabism. In the 1960s, he brought the Muslim Brotherhood to the kingdom to counter Nasserism; he also organized the Muslim World League in 1962 to challenge it throughout the Muslim world in the name of Pan-Islamic solidarity. In 1969, he convened an Islamic summit in Rabat. The summit called for a permanent Islamic organization, and in 1970 the Organization of the Islamic Conference (OIC) was established in Jiddah, where it is still functioning today.

The same year, Nasser had died and Nasserism with him. The Saudis, King Faysal in particular, remained focused on the communist threat to the Muslim world. He believed that providing schools and mosques would protect the Muslim way of life and prevent atheistic communist doctrines from overtaking the hearts and minds of Muslim youth. Thus he used these Islamic organizations as well as Saudi Islamic charitable foundations to finance the building of mosques and Islamic schools (sing. *madrasa*, plural, *madaris*) throughout the Muslim world, and the Saudi religious establishment provided teachers to run them.

With the benefit of hindsight, the Saudis have been blamed for supporting militant Wahhabism by "teaching hatred." There is a modicum of truth to the charge. Saudi teachers and imams of mosques did indeed seek to indoctrinate their listeners with radical Islamism, and this had long-term implications for the rise of militant jihadism.

But the idea that teaching puritanical Wahhabism was a premeditated Saudi policy to spread jihadism is erroneous. Militant religious indoctrination is not successful unless there is a predisposition of the recipient to find an ideological justification for venting their fears and hostility through violent acts, and although there are militant Wahhabis, the doctrine focuses primarily on tawhid, not on jihad. In short, Wahhabism and jihadism are not synonymous. More to the point, the main interest of Saudi Arabia in building schools and mosques in the Muslim world was not political indoctrination per se but rather preservation of an Islamic way of life from radical, secular Arab nationalism and atheistic communism.

It did take a long time for both Saudi Arabia and the United States, its principal partner in mutual security, to realize the long-term threat of militant jihadism. From the Saudi standpoint, one cause of the delay was the lack of oversight of Saudi programs and those of Saudi Islamic foundations. In traditional Saudi Islamic culture, the obligation of charitable giving is discharged once the gift is made. But now oversight has been put in place.

Another problem was the regime's hesitation in reining in the religious establishment. King Faysal, whose mother was an Al al-Shaykh, was well versed in Islam and not intimidated by the religious leaders. But following his death, more reactionary members of the Ulama became emboldened in seeking to preserve premodern Islamic social values and norms. In the wake of the 2003 terrorist attacks, however, King Abdullah has taken measures to create a more moderate religious leadership than in previous years.

Until the September 11 attacks, the United States showed little if any interest in Saudi Pan-Islamic policies. During the cold war, the policies were viewed as supporting the West against the Soviet Union.[7] Even the anti-Saudi campaign against the kingdom by the American Israeli lobby in the wake of the 1973 Arab-Israeli war did not attack the kingdom's Islamic policies. After 9/11, the strategic threat of jihadism and Saudi Arabia's alleged role in it became a major theme of U.S. criticism. As with the oil embargo, however, the level of mutual acrimony is subsiding with the passage of time.

Saudi Foreign Economic Policy Interests

Due to many factors, including technological advances in transportation and communications, the last quarter century has seen the evolution of a global economy. As a major oil producer, Saudi Arabia's foreign economic policies are virtually all global in scope. Ironically, its oil-based economy and thus its domestic economic welfare were global from the start. Today Saudi foreign economic interests can be divided into two overlapping categories: oil and finance..

Saudi oil interests have always been closely tied to the United States. The Americans got their oil concession in large part because the Saudis feared that European concessionaires would be followed by European colonizers. But when the first American oil men arrived in Saudi Arabia's Eastern Province in 1933, the U.S. government and the American participating companies both believed government should keep hands off of what they considered a wholly commercial venture. It was not until a decade later that direct diplomatic relations were initiated, and even then they were aimed at keeping the Saudi economy solvent until Saudi oil could be exported in appreciable amounts at the end of World War II.

Since then, Saudi-U.S. oil relations have remained major mutual interests. As outlined in chapter 4, they have also changed greatly over time and are now in the process of changing more. Whatever the future brings, however, oil relations between the two countries are likely to remain major mutual foreign economic policy interests in whatever form they take.

Another major policy interest is cooperation and coordination with other major producers in the Organization of Petroleum Exporting Countries. As the world's leading oil exporter, Saudi Arabia plays a leading role in OPEC, but it is still a consensual body, and making and abiding by consensus has often been difficult.

The two major Saudi oil policy interests are market stability and oil installation security. From the Saudi standpoint, market stability depends on the balance between aggregate production and price. There is a divide among OPEC members between those who believe the maximum return on their investment is to maintain global high prices (price hawks) and those who wish to maintain lower prices. The Saudis have always basically been price moderates. Because their whole economy is based on oil revenues, low prices can lead to serious government deficits. On the other hand, sustained high prices can lead to massive western investment in alternative sources of energy, which could ultimately collapse the market for oil.

The current minister of petroleum and mineral resources, Ali Naimi, came up through the ranks of Aramco and is fully aware of the long-term challenges for the kingdom of environmental consequences of global dependence on fossil fuels and their nonreplenishable nature, which will eventually price them out of the market. Saudi Arabia is already exploring ways to maintain the value of its major resource while making the transition to alternative sources of energy.

One of the ironies of the Saudi economy is the dependence of public sector oil revenues and its robust free-market private sector. One of the major long-term Saudi economic interests is determining overseas investment of its sizeable financial reserves. Because the United States has the largest financial market in the world, it has long maintained a major share of the Saudi investment capital, but the Saudis have also sought to diversify placement of its reserves to the extent deemed expedient.

A second Saudi interest is global investment to diversify its economy. For example, in 2008 the government announced plans to participate in a "food for security" program called the King Abdullah Initiative for Saudi Agricultural Investment Abroad. In early 2009, the kingdom announced the arrival of the first food crop harvested in foreign Saudi-owned farms.

Other Gulf countries and China have started similar programs that export capital but import food. Such programs have been heralded for providing capital, jobs, and agricultural technology to the poor, and yet they have been criticized for what is said by others to be agricultural imperialism.

From the Saudi perspective, the project accomplishes several goals. It will enable the government to phase out water-intensive production of cereal grains using nonreplenishable aquifers, provide business opportunities for the private sector while diversifying the Saudi economy, and subsidize investments of growers using aquifer water supplies.

According to the government, it will "provide credit facilities to Saudi investors in agriculture abroad," with the focus on "countries with promising agricultural resources and having encouraging government." The Islamic Development Bank was reported to be looking at investments to support agriculture, including the production of rice to be exported back to Saudi Arabia, and Ha'il Agricultural Development, a Saudi company, said in May 2009 that it would invest in agricultural production in Sudan, with the government providing 60 percent of the funding. Saudi officials have visited a number of foreign countries in Africa, Asia, and South America, and delegations from other countries have visited Saudi Arabia to discuss various investment opportunities.[8]

8

Saudi Arabia in the Twenty-first Century

Prior to the twentieth century, Saudi Arabia was one of the most conservative, traditional Islamic countries on earth. Since then, it has seen more social, economic, and political change than most western countries have experienced since the Renaissance.

Adapting to the challenges of rapid modernization has not been easy. But it has met the challenges with equanimity of what has essentially been a head-on collision of tradition and modernization. And it has done so with a minimum of the protracted social and political upheaval that generally accompanies rapid change.

For every challenge successfully met, however, new and greater challenges have taken its place. Saudi Arabia's ability to meet these challenges has largely been the result of policies that have stressed evolutionary change. Had the process not been evolutionary, the result most likely would have been a series of violent, revolutionary reactions such as have wreaked havoc in the western world for centuries. And because modernization is likely to continue, the challenges inherent in balancing it with tradition are likely to continue as well.

PROSPECTS FOR SAUDI SOCIAL DEVELOPMENT

Rapid social change is never a uniform, even process. In the kingdom, much of the social change resulting from modernization has been readily accepted. But core social values do not change rapidly, and core Islamic social values are even more impervious. If someone were to invent a time machine that could bring an eighteenth-century Najdi into the present, it would probably be only a matter of weeks before that person could become a functioning member of society, facing the onslaught of modern life with the same certitude of religious conviction with which he once faced the onslaught of enemy tribal raids. By extension, it seems reasonable to assume that core Islamic social values will continue to be shared in the future.

However, basic modern behavioral norms have and are likely to respond to the rapid changes in the environment. Perhaps the greatest existential fact of the modern Saudi social development process since the discovery of oil has been the dichotomy between the secularizing influences of modern technology and the strongly religious tradition of Saudi society. Although the two appear incompatible, most Saudis have managed surprisingly well to accept the former while clinging to the latter.

There will always be those Saudis with extreme views, however, who cannot reconcile the two, and their positions are the most visible in the West. Saudis who are frustrated about what they see as the slow pace of modernization, particularly in social development, often blame religious fanatics for being overzealous in opposing what they see as reform (including, for example, attitudes toward the role of women in society). For these Saudis, technological innovations are a gift of God to be enjoyed, and social reform is not incompatible with Islam.

For those on the far religious right, modern technology is for the most part an agent of the devil to be rejected for its corrupt, secularizing influence; social reform, they believe, is tantamount to religious innovation, which is heresy. The far religious right, however, labors under some disadvantages. It is more difficult to organize mass discontent in a conservative Islamic society against a regime whose political ideology is based on conservative Islamic values than against an avowedly secular regime. Moreover, amassing wealth is not antithetical to Islam, and a doctrine of material austerity and self-denial that many militant Islamists believe should go along with moral asceticism would find few avid followers in the kingdom's generally affluent society.

Most Saudis do not fall into either of these extremes. Highly devout people, they nevertheless have taken to technological innovation with comparative equanimity. The tension between secular modernism and religious traditionalism, however, is likely to continue well into the future and with it the potential for polarization around extremes and erosion of the center. The future direction of social development will be determined to a great extent by social trends arising from the collision of modernization and traditional culture.

As noted in chapter 3, two demographic factors have also become threats to social stability in the kingdom–rapid population growth and urbanization. The native population of Saudi Arabia has increased from 3.4 million after World War II to 22 million in 2009. This has put tremendous strain on the cohesiveness of extended families, the basic structural unit of society.

Before urbanization, most of the population mainly lived in small towns or was nomadic. They were mainly engaged in agriculture and animal husbandry. Settlement patterns were linear and spread out, but everyone knew exactly where he was from. Saudi society was traditionally shaped around a symbiosis of different lifestyles: nomadic, rural, and urban communities. By 2009, two-thirds to three-fourths of Saudis were urban.

Another result of rapid social change has been the loss of a sense of the society's cultural heritage and the rise in unsustainable economic expectations based on newly acquired oil wealth. For centuries Saudis had a strong work ethic just to survive in a harsh environment. But with the advent of modern oil wealth, many young people have taken for granted that they can have a good life with no exertion on their part. Not only have many lost their work ethic, but along with that they have lost a sense of self-fulfillment, self-esteem, and an identity based on their past.

King Abdullah has created a sort of cultural fairground at Janadriyya outside Riyadh for just that purpose: to save for future generations the arts, architecture, culture, and customs of the kingdom that were commonplace only a few decades ago. Nevertheless, many children are more familiar with the icons of Disney World than with *shi{ay}r nabati*, traditional Arabian poetry that is recited to the wail of the *al-{ay}aud* (lute) or the *rababa* (a single-stringed instrument). Future generations will be even more removed from their past.

All in all, the stresses of future shock have had a polarizing effect on Saudi society and a debilitating psychological consequence of unsustainable expectations among younger people. The great challenge for the future, therefore, is to find a balance between traditional social values and norms and modern values by maintaining what has been a successful evolutionary process of social development.

SAUDI ECONOMIC PROSPECTS

Given Saudi Arabia's huge oil reserves and the paucity of other natural resources, it is reasonable to assume that the oil sector will continue to dominate the Saudi economy and Saudi economic development strategies for some time to come. It is also reasonable to assume that the current recession and low oil prices it has created will be solved one way or another. Imprecise as those assumptions are, looking at the longer term is even more difficult to address with any degree of certainty.

The Saudi Oil Economy

Like many major global commodities, the oil market follows regular business cycles, and at some point the market is virtually certain to shift dramatically. With the low oil prices brought on by the recession of 2009, that might seem like good news for the Saudis, but over the longer term it is a mixed blessing. Oil is a nonreplenishable commodity, and at some time in the future, most likely in the present century, global productive capacity is likely to be overtaken by global demand pricing oil out of the market as alternative sources become more competitive. In addition, the advance of global warming is likely to reduce the salability of oil and other fossil fuels as the leading sources of carbon emissions.

These rather stark assumptions present both the Saudi oil-based economy and its economic development strategies with both short-term and long-term challenges. Strategies to address them, however, are not necessarily compatible. Faced with lower revenues, the kingdom is likely to cancel or at least postpone planned capital investment in oil production. In the long run, that could well lead to another spike in prices once the recession is over, and this could lead to another collapse in prices as investment in alternative energy sources becomes more competitive.

Early but not massive capital investment in alternative energy sources would be in the Saudis' best interests and indeed the global economy's interests. And the Saudis have taken steps to look into such investments. But even in a booming economy they cannot do it alone. Their best hope is if awareness of the long-term challenge in global energy will increase sooner rather than later.

Prospects for Economic Development

With the exception of the hajj service industry, which now operates year-round and employs thousands of people, the Saudi oil-based economy, including producing, refining, and using oil and gas as feed stocks for fertilizer plants and plastics, is to a great extent capital-intensive. In the early years of the oil era, expatriates ran much of the production, and even today there are some 5 million expatriates in the kingdom, ranging from senior executives and bankers to unskilled labor.

Economic plans in those days concentrated on physical infrastructure and education, which is predominantly free through the university level. The country has passed that stage, however, and is now concentrating more on expanding and diversifying the economy, providing employment for Saudi nationals, and planning for the post-oil era.

Saudi human resources have grown almost exponentially over the past 40 years and have become one of the country's greatest economic resources. However, the productivity of young Saudi males is simply not competitive with foreign laborers who will work for lower wages. Saudi women, on the other hand, have a far greater work ethic and are more determined to expand their education and marketable skills. There are now more female college graduates than male graduates. Current social practice, however, bans them from being in contact with males in the workplace, so those who are employed work in fields where they need only meet other women.

There is another cultural element that has been all but unnoticed. Saudi Arabia's traditional patriarchal society has always stressed respect for elders, and by extension this has reserved for elders the principal role in decision making. The extended life expectancy has enabled them to maintain this role far longer than in the past, and with the exception of major industrial personnel, the accompanying reluctance of many elders to delegate authority is increasingly depriving the workforce of middle managers being groomed for senior positions.

When looking to the future, when the oil-based economy will begin to shrink, human resources could become one of the country's greatest assets. But in order for that to occur, more efficient use of males and females will be mandatory. The social obstacles are great and cannot be overcome quickly. For the labor force to be more skilled, more motivated, and broader based, change must carefully evolve.

PROSPECTS FOR SAUDI POLITICAL DEVELOPMENT

The Executive Branch

It is difficult for many westerners to visualize the Saudi monarchy as anything but a medieval dictatorship in the absence of a national elective political process for choosing a chief executive or an elective representative parliament that chooses the head of government. It is certainly not democratic in the western sense. But the king is not above the law. The Islamic constitutional system of Saudi Arabia is supreme and cannot be amended.

In addition, there has always been public participation in the political process, particularly in the Najdi heartland. The traditional means of legitimizing group decisions, in the family and in business as well as in government, is through *shura* (consultation) in order to create a consensus. Thus the king is not only the chief executive but also the chief consensus maker. It is a process that has been sanctified in Islamic law and is deeply ingrained in the culture.

Barring some cataclysmic set of circumstances, the monarchy is likely to retain its legitimacy in the foreseeable future. On more than one occasion, however, there has been a lack of consensus over succession. In recent times, succession has been passed down to the sons of King Abd al-Aziz according to seniority, experience, and ability. Islam calls for the monarch to be physically, mentally, and morally able to rule.

With the sons now reaching old age, the time is approaching when succession must be passed down to the next generation of Abd al-Aziz's descendents. This could be a challenging and potentially even dangerous time for the regime if a consensus is not reached on whom that will be. The primary consensus makers will be the royal family itself, and in 2006 King Abdullah created the Bay{ay}ah (Allegiance) Council of sons and grandsons of Abd al-Aziz to ensure a smooth transition. In addition, there is an ancient consensus-making institution known as Ahl al-{ay} Aqd wal al-Hall (people who bind and loosen), which also includes recognized leaders of the entire country.

Public Participation in the Political Process

Western notions of public participation include not only an elected head of government but also an elected representative legislature. Despite the absence of a formal democratic process, traditional Saudi society has always played a participatory role in the political process. Although public participation is to a great degree a reflection of collective loyalties based on extended family, tribal, sectarian, and regional affiliations, it is also a highly individual activity. Saudi political culture was (and continues to be) highly individualistic and egalitarian. In the past, political leaders held a regular, informal *majlis* (assembly) where individuals could come and petition for aid, submit grievances, and express views on given issues. Although the complexities and reach of modern government have to some extent limited the practice, it has still survived to a significant extent.

Rapid modernization has increasingly required a more institutionalized process of participation. In the 1920s, King Abd al-Aziz sought to expand the formal Hijazi Majlis al-Shura (Consultative Council) to the entire kingdom, but he was turned down by the religious establishment in Riyadh. Though it was an ancient Islamic institution, the religious leaders opposed it as a nascent legislature that they considered heretical because Islamic law cannot be amended. It was never formally abolished but remained dormant until 1992, when King Fahd revived a nationwide Majlis al-Shura, to be made up of recognized professional leaders throughout the country. The Majlis was convened for the first time in 1993.

News of the revival met with mixed reactions at home and abroad. Those calling for more rapid political reform were critical because its members were appointed rather than elected. Others were more positive because they saw it as the first step toward a representative public participation in the political process. Many westerners saw it as the first step toward a national legislature, but were ignorant of or else ignored the fact that Islamic law is immutable and cannot be amended.

The traditional function of a majlis al-shura is formal, representative consultation leading to consensus, which legitimizes governmental decisions. And as such, the Saudi Majlis has emerged as an effective institution in legitimizing public government policymaking. Its influence is evidenced by the expanding efforts of the government ministries to seek its consensus and avoid consensus contrary to their interests.

In 2005, King Abdullah called for municipal elections. Only men were allowed to vote, and again, there were those inside and outside the country who wanted the process to change at a faster pace. However, the pace has successfully met the balance between the need for change and the need to preserve.

Demands will undoubtedly be made for more public participation in the political process by future generations as complex issues arise, many of them defying solution or beyond the control of the government to influence in a meaningful way. Public participation in the political process is thus likely to be the key to the direction that long-term Saudi political development will take.

The Evolution of Governmental Institutions

The evolution toward more modern governmental institutions could be said to have begun when Abd al-Aziz took and annexed the Hijaz in the 1920s. The Hijaz have a consultative assembly and formal governmental institutions, including cabinet ministers and ministries. Abd al-Aziz immediately began to expand the reach of these institutions nationwide, and he and his successors created new ministries and agencies as the need was perceived.

Building the basic modern institutional infrastructure has for the most part been completed. Bureaucracies and staffs to fill them have been created to address the entire breadth of governmental responsibilities. New institutions have been created as the need arises, but the main challenges for the future are more likely to focus on increasing productivity. One challenge is to create the most efficient organizational structures possible within ministries and agencies to carry out their assigned duties. A second challenge is to increase the efficiency of government personnel. After World War II, the first generation of Saudis getting a modern college education were virtually guaranteed a government position. As the educational system has expanded, that is no longer the case. Productivity is not based on a college degree alone. Like the private sector, instilling a higher standard of performance among government personnel requires a higher degree of self-discipline and an enhanced work ethic. It also requires greater managerial skills, such as the delegation of authority and interoffice and interagency cooperation in addressing issues in which no single office or agency has sole responsibility. It should be borne in mind, however, that increasing the efficiency of Saudi public administration is an ongoing process and cannot be achieved in a day.

In sum, the most likely direction of political development in Saudi Arabia is evolutionary rather than revolutionary. Nevertheless, when such changes are gradual, it is always a good idea periodically to test one's underlying assumptions, for conditions in this part of the world can change rapidly and without warning.

PROSPECTS FOR SAUDI NATIONAL SECURITY

The evolution of Saudi national security threats and efforts to meet them have been every bit as great as all the other changes that have occurred. The rise of the Wahhabi Saudi state and its expansion in the eighteenth and nineteenth centuries led plausibly to the first foreign power invasion in the history of Najd. Later in the nineteenth century, the Al Saud regime collapsed and was replaced by an Al Rashid regime from Ha{ha}il. During World War I, the Saudis looked to Britain, the predominant western power in the region, for security. Despite Britain's similar relationship with the Hijaz, Abd al-Aziz invaded and annexed it in the 1920s in reaction to the Hijazi king, Sharif Hussein of Makkah, and then declared himself the caliph of Sunni Islam.

During that entire period, military material was constantly upgraded, but battles were fought in the traditional, premodern way by camelborne tribal levies. The last Bedouin battle in history was fought in 1929 at Sibilla between tribes loyal to Abd al-Aziz and those in rebellion. Both sides had camel cavalries, but Abd al-Aziz also had the advantage of motor vehicles and aircraft flown by British pilots.

It was the end of an era. After the war and because of the cold war that followed, the king was convinced that much as he distrusted a standing army, the kingdom needed a modern armed force. In 1945 the United States and the United Kingdom began to help the Saudis create one. At the same time, the kingdom diversified its national security portfolio for training and arms sales to include a number of other countries.

Although the United States remained the principal ally for arms supplies and training over the years, the bilateral relationship was often strained, particularly after 1973 when the U.S. Israel lobby became concerned that the United States might downgrade its support to Israel for a secure supply of Saudi oil. Even so, the Saudi armed forces continued to improve and acquitted themselves well during Operation Desert Storm against Iraq in 1991.

Ironically, from a national security perspective, Desert Storm was the end of another era, one in which virtually all national security threats were viewed in terms of conventional warfare. But since 1991, the predominant national security threats to Saudi Arabia have been asymmetrical—terrorism and insurgencies.

Saudi responses to asymmetrical threats that have risen since Desert Storm have on the whole been effective. They have included not only the armed services, particularly special operations, but also law enforcement and internal security services, diplomacy, and public relations. Most notable has been the Saudi rehabilitation program. Seasoned terrorist veterans are not likely to be won over by such a program, but it has been very successful with young people who have become recruits of asymmetrical groups out of anger, fear, or grievance.

LOOKING TO THE FUTURE

Seeking to guess the future is always a difficult if not futile action. It is even more difficult in an environment of such uncertainty as the world of today. Finding one's way through unchartered territory is always filled with risk and unknown consequences. But the record of Saudi Arabia in surviving unparalleled social, economic, and political change in the face of unprecedented modernization, and doing so while holding fast to its basic values and norms, is remarkable. It has been the theme throughout this book that its past success in doing so was based on the measured, evolutionary process it has followed. It seems logical therefore to assume that whatever future challenges it may encounter, continuing this process is the viable option from which to choose.

Appendix

SELECTED GENEALOGY OF THE AL SAUD

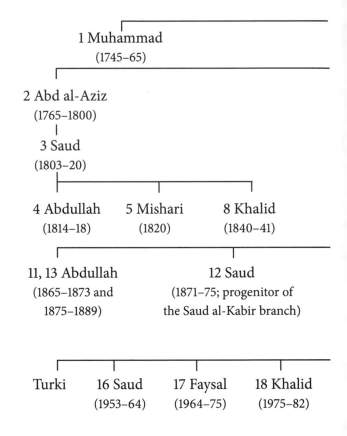

1 Muhammad
(1745–65)

2 Abd al-Aziz
(1765–1800)

3 Saud
(1803–20)

4 Abdullah   5 Mishari   8 Khalid
(1814–18)   (1820)   (1840–41)

11, 13 Abdullah   12 Saud
(1865–1873 and   (1871–75; progenitor of
1875–1889)   the Saud al-Kabir branch)

Turki   16 Saud   17 Faysal   18 Khalid
           (1953–64)   (1964–75)   (1975–82)

Note: Numbers, bold type, and dates indicate rulers and the period of their reigns.

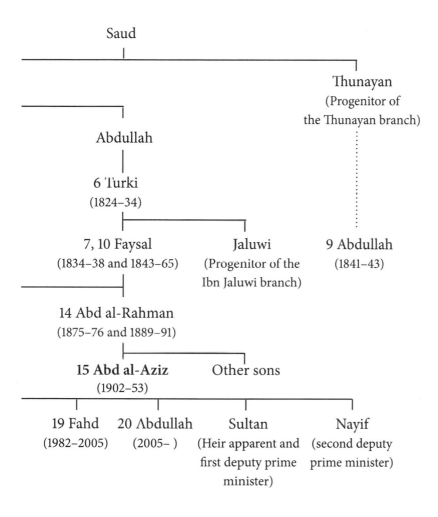

Saud

Thunayan
(Progenitor of
the Thunayan branch)

Abdullah

6 Turki
(1824–34)

7, 10 Faysal
(1834–38 and 1843–65)

Jaluwi
(Progenitor of the
Ibn Jaluwi branch)

9 Abdullah
(1841–43)

14 Abd al-Rahman
(1875–76 and 1889–91)

15 Abd al-Aziz
(1902–53)

Other sons

19 Fahd
(1982–2005)

20 Abdullah
(2005–)

Sultan
(Heir apparent and
first deputy prime
minister)

Nayif
(second deputy
prime minister)

Table 2. Number of Pilgrims on Hajj, 1996–2008/1416–1428

Year	Total	Saudis	Non-Saudis
1416/1996	1,865,234	784,769	1,080,465
1417/1997	1,942,851	774,260	1,168,591
1418/1998	1,832,114	699,770	1,132,344
1419/1999	1,831,998	775,268	1,056,730
1420/2000	1,839,154	571,599	1,267,555
1421/2001	1,913,263	549,271	1,363,992
1422/2002	1,944,760	590,576	1,354,184
1423/2003	2,041,129	610,117	1,431,012
1424/2004	2,012,074	592,368	1,419,706
1425/2005	2,164,469	629,710	1,534,769
1426/2006	2,130,594	573,147	1,557,447
1427/2007	2,454,325	747,000	1,707,325
1428/2008	2,408,849	679,008	1,729,841

Table 3. Development of Average World Oil Prices

Year	Average Price per Barrel in U.S. Dollars
January 1996	18.41
January 1997	23.18
January 1998	15.21
January 1999	9.76
January 2000	23.17
January 2001	22.10
January 2002	18.68
January 2003	29.03
January 2004	28.00
January 2005	35.16
January 2006	55.12
January 2007	54.63
January 2008	92.93
January 2009	34.57

Source: U.S. Energy Information Administration.

Notes

Chapter 1. The Land and People

1. Makkah and al-Madinah are the official Saudi English spellings according to the Saudi Ministry of Information.

2. For an interesting account by one of the first outsiders to traverse the area, see Thesiger, *Arabian Sands*.

3. Translation provided by George Rentz, quoted in Twitchell, *Saudi Arabia*, 8.

4. David E. Long, Personal Papers.

5. Ibid.

Chapter 2. Historical Background

1. See the bibliography for books by Philby, Burton, Doughty, Ibn Bishr, and Ibn Ghannam.

2. *Shaykh* (also transliterated as *sheikh*, *sheikh*, and *sheik*) is an all-purpose Arabic word denoting respect. It can mean a teacher, a tribal leader, an important person, or simply a grand old man.

3. According to Philby, he belonged to the Masharifa clan of the Bani Tamim tribe. See Philby, *Arabia*, 8–12.

4. For a discussion of Ibn Taymiyya's views, see Nettler, "Ibn Taymiyyah," in Esposito, ed., *The Oxford Encyclopedia of the Modern Islamic World*, 2:165–66. His life is discussed in Williams, ed., *Islam*.

5. Winder, *Saudi Arabia in the Nineteenth Century*, 228

6. There are a number of good popular books containing biographical information on King Abd al-Aziz, including Armstrong, *Lord of Arabia*, De Gaury, *Arabia Phoenix*, Howarth, *The Desert King*, and the works of Philby. Two scholarly studies of this period are Helms, *The Cohesion of Saudi Arabia*, and Kostiner, *The Making of Saudi Arabia, 1916–1936*.

7. Philby, *Arabia*, 160.

8. For an analysis of the Ikhwan, see Habib, *Ibn Saʿudʾs Warriors of Islam*.

9. For a description of the early constitutional and bureaucratic developments of the kingdom, see Davies, *The Organization of the Government of Saudi Arabia*.

10. One of the better biographies of King Faysalʾs early years is De Gaury, *Faysal*. Recently, two scholarly biographies, Kechichianʾs *Faysal: Saudi Arabiaʾs King for All Seasons*, and Vassilievʾs *King Faisal of Saudi Arabia*, are recommended readings.

11. David E. Long, Personal Papers. The ambassador was Hermann Eilts.

12. See al-Zaydi, "King Abdullahʾs Vision for Saudi Arabia."

Chapter 3. Tradition and Modernization

1. Many of the ideas discussed in this chapter are drawn from Long, *The Culture and Customs of Saudi Arabia*, chapter 2.

2. David E. Long, Personal Papers.

3. The Jaʿfari school, named after Jaʿfar al-Sadiq, the sixth Shiʿa Imam, diverges in some instances from Sunni schools, but in substance the differences are not major.

4. For an interesting eighteenth-century account of Jiddah, the commercial center of the Hijaz, see Niebuhr, *Travels through Arabia and Other Countries in the East*.

5. David E. Long, Personal Papers.

6. For a discussion of the health aspects of the hajj, see Long, *The Hajj Today*.

7. Armerding, *Doctors for the Kingdom*, 13.

8. In the wake of the September 11 terrorist attacks, longtime U.S. critics of Saudi Arabia inter alia sought to link the Saudi government with terrorism by claiming that its educational system taught "race hatred" based on Islam, both at home and in Saudi schools in the United States. In response, the Saudis excised some more inflammatory prose, but apparently no editing could satisfy the critics. Ironically, hostility is not learned from a text. According to social psychology, the root causes hostility are fear and grievance.

9. See Ochsenwald, *The Hijaz Railroad*.

10. See, for example, Long, "King Faisalʾs World View."

Chapter 4. Oil and Saudi Arabia

1. U.S. Central Intelligence Agency, *The CIA World Factbook, 2009*.

2. DeNovo, "The Movement for Aggressive American Oil Policy Abroad, 1918–1920."

3. See Stocking, *Middle East Oil*. A more popularized although extensively researched account is Yergin, *The Prize*.

4. For a discussion of these events, see Stocking, *Middle East Oil*, 40–65.

5. Long, *The United States and Saudi Arabia*, 13.

6. For an account of the founding and early days of Aramco, see Nawwab, Speers, and Hoye, eds., *Aramco and Its World*, 188–97; Barger, *Out of the Blue*; and Stegner, *Discovery*.

7. For the text of the declaration, see U.S. Department of State, *Foreign Relations of the United States, 1943*, 854.

8. Mikesell, *Foreign Investment in the Petroleum and Mineral Industries*, 220.

9. See Yergin, *The Prize*, 519–27.

10. For an analysis of this period, see Weisberg, *The Politics of Crude Oil Pricing in the Middle East, 1970–1975*.

11. Long, *The United States and Saudi Arabia*, 24–25.

12. U.S. Department of State, "The Evolution of OPEC, 1959–1983," 10–11.

13. Long, *The United States and Saudi Arabia*, 28.

14. Based on figures from the American embassy in Riyadh and the Riyadh Bank.

15. U.S. Department of Energy, Energy Information Administration, *World Crude Prices*, October 2008.

16. "Saudi Capacity Could Reach 15 Million B/D," *Platts Oilgram News* 86, no. 128 (July 1, 2008): 1.

17. Bloomberg Energy Prices, January 5, 2009, Bloomberg.com/energy.

18. U.S. Department of Energy, Energy Information Administration, *Spot Market Prices for Crude Oil and Petroleum Products*, June 17, 2009, http://tonto.eia.doe.gov/dnav/pet/pet_pri_spt_s1_d.htm.

19. Ie.d4

20. See "Seeing Oil's Limits, Gulf States Invest Heavily in the Clean Energy," *Washington Post*, January 13, 2009, A1.

Chapter 5. Economic Development and Modernization

1. The word *riba* means "gain" or "increase," but generally it refers to charges for extending loans or credit. See Ray, *Arab Islamic Banking and the Renewal of Islamic Law*.

2. For an account of the creation of the banking system, see Ali, *Saudi Arabian Monetary Agency*, 118–30.

3. Material in this section is drawn in part from Young, *Saudi Arabia: The Making of a Financial Giant*.

4. Royal Decree No. 30/4/1/1046, dated 25/7/1371 (April 20, 1952), *Umm al-Qura*, 3/8/1371 (27/4/1952), cited in Ali, *Saudi Arabian Monetary Agency*, 26–27.

5. Thomas W. Shea, "The Riyal: A Miracle in Money," *Aramco World*, January/February 1969, quoted in Ali, *Saudi Arabian Monetary Agency*, 77.

6. U.S. Central Intelligence Agency, *The CIA World Factbook, 2009*.

7. Ray, *Arab Islamic Banking*, 6–7.

8. See www.hajinformation.com/main/y1949.htm.

Chapter Six. The Saudi Political System

1. Bill, "The Plasticity of Informal Politics."

2. David E. Long, Personal Papers.

3. For a description of the early constitutional and bureaucratic development of Saudi Arabia, see Davies, *The Organization of the Government of Saudi Arabia*.

4. Fatwa of February 11, 1927, quoted in ibid., 33. The Arabic text is found in Wahba, *Jazirat al-'Arab fil-Qarn al-'Ashrin*.   5. Independent public agencies include economic bodies (Royal Commission for Jubayl and Yanbu), educational institutions (public universities), social welfare agencies (Red Crescent), and the central bank (Saudi Arabian Monetary Fund).

6. The term *amir* (*emir*), like *shaykh*, has multiple meanings. It can connote a male member of a ruling family (the female term is *amira*) but can also mean the leader of an amirate, which can be an independent state, a member of a federation, or a province of a larger state, which is the case here. Here, amir/amirate is used to describe a Saudi provincial leader/province or member of the Saudi royal family. Emir/emirate refers to an independent ruler/state on the Persian Gulf.

7. Text of the "Royal Decree on the Regions Statute, Kingdom of Saudi Arabia," translated by Foreign Broadcast Information Service, London, March 1, 1992.

8. For a detailed account on the structure of the judiciary of the kingdom, see Ansary, *A Brief Overview of the Saudi Arabian Legal System*.

9. See, for example, Henderson, *After King Fahd: Succession in Saudi Arabia*, and Kechichian, *Succession in Saudi Arabia*.

10. See Awadh Al-Badi, "Institutionalising Hereditary Succession in Saudi Arabia's Political Governance System: The Allegiance Commission," *Arab Reform Initiative*, Arab Reform Brief 20, http://arab-reform.net/IMG/pdf/ARB_20_A.Saoudite_A.AL_Badi_ENG.pdf.

11. See Long, *The Hajj Today*.

12. See Ochsenwald, *The Hijaz Railroad*.

13. Long, "The Impact of the Iranian Revolution on the Arabian Peninsula and the Gulf States," 108–9.

14. Meulen, *The Wells of Ibn Sa'ud*, 121.

Chapter 7. Saudi Foreign and National Security Policies

1. For a fuller development of these themes, see Long, "King Faisal's World View."

2. For a discussion of the classical Islamic worldview, see Khadduri, *The Islamic Law of Nations*.

3. See Eddy, *F.D.R. Meets Ibn Saud*.

4. For an account of Saudi military development and the U.S. role in it, see Long, *The United States and Saudi Arabia*, 33–72; Cordesman, *The Gulf and the Search for Strategic Stability*; and Cordesman, *The Gulf and the West*.

5. *Washington Post*, November 14, 1995, A1.

6. Ashura, the 10th of Muharram on the Islamic calendar, commemorates the martyrdom of Husayn bin Ali, who was killed by the Sunni caliph Yazid bin Muawiya in the battle of Karbala in 680.

7. In the early 1970s, David Long, who was assigned to the U.S. State Department's Bureau of Intelligence and Research, tried in vain to interest senior officials in the Islamic concept of Dar al-Islam and Dar al-Harb. He wrote an analysis that suggested that if the cold war ever ended, the United States could replace the Soviet Union as the new Dar al-Harb in the eyes of politically disaffected Arabs and Muslims due to its pro-Israeli policies and its modern secular culture. The analysis was considered not "policy relevant" and was never published. In the throes of the cold war, there was simply no interest in Islamic political theory. David E. Long, Personal Papers.

8. Javier Blas, "Saudis Get First Taste of Foreign Harvest," *Financial Times*, March 5, 2009; *Economist*, May 21, 2009.

Selected Bibliography

Abir, Mordechai. *Saudi Arabia: Government, Society, and the Gulf Crisis.* London: Routledge, 1993.

Ali, Mohammad Said AlHaj. *Saudi Arabian Monetary Agency: A Review of Its Accomplishments, 1372–1411 AH/1952–1991 AD.* Riyadh: Saudi Arabian Ministry of Information, Safar 1412/August 1991.

Ansary, Abdullah F. *A Brief Overview of the Saudi Arabian Legal System.* New York: Hauser Global Law School Program, New York University School of Law, 2008.

Armerding, Paul L. *Doctors for the Kingdom: The Work of the American Mission Hospital in the Kingdom of Saudi Arabia, 1913–1955.* Grand Rapids, Mich.: Eerdmans, 2003.

Armstrong, H. C. *Lord of Arabia.* London: Baker, 1934.

Badeeb, Saeed M. *The Saudi-Egyptian Conflict over North Yemen, 1962–1970.* Boulder, Colo.: Westview, 1986.

Barger, Thomas C. *Out of the Blue: Letters from Arabia, 1937–1940.* Vista, Calif.: Selwa Press, 2002.

Baroody, George M. "The Practice of Law in Saudi Arabia." In *King Faisal and the Modernisation of Saudi Arabia*, ed. William A. Beling. London: Croom Helm; Boulder, Colo.: Westview, 1980.

Beling, William A., ed. *King Faisal and the Modernisation of Saudi Arabia.* London: Croom Helm; Boulder, Colo.: Westview, 1980.

Bill, James A. "The Plasticity of Informal Politics: The Case of Iran." *Middle East Journal* 27 (Spring 1973): 131–51.

Binduqji, Husayn Hamza [Bindagji, Hussein H.]. *Jughrafiyat al-Mamlaka al-'Arabiyya al-Sa'udiyya* [The geography of Saudi Arabia]. Cairo: Maktabat Anjalu Masriyya, 1397/1977.

Burton, Richard F. *Personal Narrative of a Pilgrimage to al-Madinah and Meccah.* 2 vols. London: Bell, 1898.

Cordesman, Anthony. *The Gulf and the Search for Strategic Stability: Saudi Arabia, the Military Balance in the Gulf, and Trends in the Arab-Israeli Military Balance.* Boulder, Colo.: Westview; London: Mansell, 1984.

———. *The Gulf and the West.* Boulder, Colo.: Westview, 1988.

———. *Saudi Arabia Enters the Twenty-first Century.* Westport, Conn.: Praeger, 2003.

———. "Saudi Military Forces in the 1990s: The Strategic Challenge of Continued Modernization." Paper delivered at "Inside Saudi Arabia: Society, Economy, and Security," a conference of the Royal Institute of International Affairs in cooperation with the Middle East Association, London, October 4–5, 1993.

Cordesman, Anthony, and Nawaf E. Obaid. *National Security in Saudi Arabia: Threats, Responses, and Challenges.* Westport, Conn.: Praeger, 2005.

Coulson, N. J. *A History of Islamic Law.* Edinburgh: Edinburgh University Press, 1964, 1971.

Davies, Roger. *The Organization of the Government of Saudi Arabia.* Jiddah, Saudi Arabia: American Legation, 1948.

Dawisha, Adeed I. *Saudi Arabia's Search for Security.* Adelphi Paper no. 158. London: International Institute for Strategic Studies, Winter 1979–80.

De Gaury, Gerald. *Arabia Phoenix.* London: Harrap, 1946.

———. *Faysal: King of Saudi Arabia.* New York: Praeger, 1966.

Dekmejian, R. Hrair. "The Rise of Political Islamism in Saudi Arabia." *Middle East Journal* 48 (Autumn 1994): 627–43.

Delong-Bas, Natana. *Wahhabi Islam: From Revival and Reform to Global Jihad.* New York: Oxford University Press, 2004.

DeNovo, John. "The Movement for Aggressive American Oil Policy Abroad, 1918–1920." *American Historical Review* 61 (July 1956): 854–76.

Doran, Charles F., and Stephen W. Buck, eds. *The Gulf, Energy, and Global Security: Political and Economic Issues.* Boulder, Colo.: Lynne Rienner, 1991.

Doughty, Charles M. *Travels in Arabia Deserta.* Cambridge: Cambridge University Press, 1888.

Eddy, William. *F.D.R. Meets Ibn Saud.* New York: American Friends of the Middle East, 1954.

Esposito, John L., ed. *The Iranian Revolution: Its Global Impact.* Miami: Florida International Press, 1990.

———. *Islam: The Straight Path.* New York: Oxford University Press, 1988.

———, ed. *Voices of Resurgent Islam.* New York: Oxford University Press, 1983.

Al-Farsy, Fouad. *Modernity and Tradition: The Saudi Equation.* London: Kegan Paul International, 1990.

Gauze, F. Gregory. *Saudi-Yemeni Relations: Domestic Structures and Foreign Influence.* New York: Columbia University Press, 1990.

Grunebaum, Gustave E. von. *Muhammadan Festivals*. New York: Henry Schuman, 1951.

Habib, John S. *Ibn Sa'ud's Warriors of Islam: The Ikhwan of Najd and Their Role in the Creation of the Sa'udi Kingdom, 1910–1930*. Leiden: Brill, 1978.

Hamza, Fuad. *Al-Bilad al-'Arabiyya al-Sa'udiyya* [The land of Saudi Arabia]. Riyadh: Maktabat al-Nasr al-Haditha, 1968.

Helms, Christine Moss. *The Cohesion of Saudi Arabia*. Baltimore: Johns Hopkins University Press, 1981.

Henderson, Simon. *After King Fahd: Succession in Saudi Arabia*. Washington: Washington Institute for Near East Policy, 1994.

Henry, Clement M., and Rodney Wilson, eds. *The Politics of Islamic Finance*. Edinburgh: Edinburgh University Press, 2004.

Holden, David. *Farewell to Arabia*. London: Faber, 1966.

Holden, David, and Richard Johns. *The House of Saud*. New York: Holt, Rinehart and Winston, 1982.

Howarth, David. *The Desert King: Ibn Sa'ud and His Arabia*. New York: McGraw-Hill, 1964.

Huyette, Summer Scott. *Political Adaptation in Saudi Arabia*. Boulder, Colo.: Westview, 1985.

Ibn Bishr, Uthman. *Unwan al-Majd fi Tarikh Najd* [Chapters of the glory in the history of Najd]. Riyadh: Dar Banna lil Tiba'a wa Tajlid, 1953.

Ibn Ghannam, Husayn. *Rawdhat al-Afkar wal Afham: Tarikh Najd* [A garden of meditations and understandings: The history of Najd]. Riyadh: al-Maktabah al-Ahliyyah, 1949.

Ibn Taymiyyah, Taqi al-Din Ahmad. *Al-Siyasa al-Shariiyyah* [Islamic politics]. Beirut: Dar al-Kutub al-Arabiyyah, 1966.

Johany, Ali D. *The Myth of the OPEC Cartel: The Role of Saudi Arabia*. New York: Wiley, 1982.

Kechichian, Joseph. *Faysal: Saudi Arabia's King for All Seasons*. Gainesville: University Press of Florida, 2008.

———. *Succession in Saudi Arabia*. London: Palgrave Macmillan, 2003.

Khadduri, Majid. *The Islamic Law of Nations: Shaybani's Siyar*. Baltimore: Johns Hopkins University Press, 1966.

Kostiner, Joseph. *The Making of Saudi Arabia, 1916–1936: From Chieftaincy to Monarchical State*. New York: Oxford University Press, 1993.

Krimly, Rayed Khalid. "The Political Economy of Rentier States: A Case Study of Saudi Arabia in the Oil Era." PhD diss., George Washington University, 1993.

Lacey, Robert. *The Kingdom*. London: Hutcheson, 1981.

Lees, Bryan. *A Handbook of the Al Saud Ruling Family of Saudi Arabia*. London: Royal Genealogies, 1980.

Long, David E. *Culture and Customs of Saudi Arabia*. Westport, Conn.: Greenwood Press, 2005.

———. *The Hajj Today: A Survey of the Contemporary Pilgrimage to Makkah*. Albany: State University of New York Press, 1979.

———. "The Impact of the Iranian Revolution on the Arabian Peninsula and the Gulf States." In *The Iranian Revolution: Its Global Impact*, ed. John L. Esposito. Miami: Florida International University Press, 1990.

———. "King Faisal's World View." In *King Faisal and the Modernisation of Saudi Arabia*, ed. Willard A. Beling, 173–83. London: Croom Helm; Boulder, Colo.: Westview, 1980.

———. *Saudi Arabia*. Washington Papers 4, no. 39. Beverly Hills: Sage, 1976.

———. "Saudi Arabia and Its Neighbors: Preoccupied Paternalism." *In Crosscurrents in the Gulf*, ed. Richard Sindelar and J. E. Peterson for the Middle East Institute. London: Routledge, 1988.

———. "Saudi Arabia in the 1990s: Plus Ça Change." In *The Gulf, Energy, and Global Security: Political and Economic Issues*, ed. Charles F. Doran and Stephen W. Buck. Boulder, Colo.: Lynne Rienner, 1991.

———. "Saudi Foreign Policy and the Arab-Israeli Peace Process: The Fahd (Arab) Peace Plan." In *Middle East Peace Plans*, ed. Willard A. Beling. London: Croom Helm, 1986.

———. *The United States and Saudi Arabia: Ambivalent Allies*. Boulder, Colo.: Westview, 1985.

Maisel, Sebastian. *Das Gewohnheitsrecht der Beduinen* [The customary law of the Bedouins]. Frankfurt: Lang, 2006.

Maisel, Sebastian, and John Shoup. *Saudi Arabia and Gulf States Today*. Westport, Conn.: Greenwood, 2009.

Meulen, D. van der. *The Wells of Ibn Sa'ud*. New York: Praeger, 1957.

Mikesell, Raymond F., ed. *Foreign Investment in the Petroleum and Mineral Industries*. Baltimore: Johns Hopkins University Press, 1971.

Nallino, Carlo Alfonso. *L'Arabia Saudiana*. Vol. 1 of *Raccolta di scritti editi e inediti*, ed. Maria Nallino. Rome: Istituto per l'Oriente, 1939.

Nawwab, Ismail, Peter Speers, and Paul F. Hoye, eds. *Aramco and Its World: Arabia and the Middle East*. Washington: Arabian American Oil Company, 1980.

Nettler, Ronald. "Ibn Taymiyya." In *The Oxford Encyclopedia of the Modern Islamic World*, 4 vols., ed. John L. Esposito, 2:165–66. New York: Oxford University Press, 1995.

Niebuhr, Carsten. *Travels through Arabia and Other Countries in the East*. Trans. Robert Heron. 1792; Reading: Garnet, 1994.

Nyang, Sulayman, and Evan Hendricks. *A Line in the Sand: Saudi Arabia's Role in the Gulf War*. Washington: P.T. Books, 1995.

Ochsenwald, William. *The Hijaz Railroad*. Charlottesville: University of Virginia Press, 1980.

———. *Religion, Society, and the State in Arabia: The Hijaz under Ottoman Control, 1849–1908*. Columbus: Ohio State University Press, 1984.

Painter, David S. *Oil and the American Century*. Baltimore: Johns Hopkins University Press, 1986.

Peters, F. E. *The Hajj: The Muslim Pilgrimage to Mecca and the Holy Places*. Princeton: Princeton University Press, 1994.

Peterson, Erik R. *The Gulf Cooperation Council: Search for Unity in a Dynamic Region*. Boulder, Colo.: Westview, 1988.

Philby, H. St. John B. *Arabia*. London: Benn, 1930.

———. *Arabia of the Wahhabis*. London: Constable, 1928.

———. *Arabian Days: An Autobiography*. London: Hale, 1948.

———. *Arabian Jubilee*. London: Hale, 1952.

———. *Arabian Oil Ventures*. Washington: Middle East Institute, 1964.

———. *Sa'udi Arabia*. New York: Arno, 1972.

Al-Rasheed, Madawi. *A History of Saudi Arabia*. Cambridge University Press, 2002.

Ray, Nicholas Dylan. *Arab Islamic Banking and the Renewal of Islamic Law*. Boston: Graham and Trotman, 1995.

Rihani, Ameen. *Ibn Sa'oud of Arabia*. London: Constable, 1928.

Shaw, John A., and David E. Long. *Saudi Arabian Modernization: The Impact of Change on Stability*. Washington Papers 10, no. 89. New York: Praeger, 1982.

Stegner, Wallace. *Discovery: The Search for Arabian Oil*. Portola, Calif.: Selwa Press, 2007.

Stocking, George W. *Middle East Oil: A Study in Political and Economic Controversy*. Nashville: Vanderbilt University Press, 1970.

Sultan, Khaled bin, with Patrick Seale. *Desert Warrior: A Personal View of the Gulf War by the Joint Forces Commander*. New York: HarperCollins, 1995.

Thesiger, Wilfred. *Arabian Sands*. London: Readers Union/Longman, 1960.

Twitchell, Karl S. *Saudi Arabia: With an Account of the Development of Its Natural Resources*. 3d ed. New York: Greenwood, 1958.

U.S. Central Intelligence Agency. *The CIA World Factbook*. New York: Skyhorse, 2009

U.S. Department of Energy, Energy Information Administration. *World Crude Prices*, October 2008.

U.S. Department of State. *Foreign Relations of the United States, 1943*. Vol. 4. Washington: Government Printing Office, 1943.

U.S. Department of State. Office of the Historian. "The Evolution of OPEC, 1959–1983." Historical Research Project no. 1349 (n.d.).

Vassiliev, Alexei. *The History of Saudi Arabia*. London: Al Saqi, 1998.

———. *King Faisal of Saudi Arabia*. London: Al Saqi, 2009.

Wahba, Hafiz. *Arabian Days*. London: Barker, 1964.

———. *Jazirat al-'Arab fil-Qarn al-'Ashrin* [The Arabian peninsula in the twentieth century]. Cairo: Matba'at al-Nahdah al-Misriyyah, 1961.

Watt, W. Montgomery. *Free Will and Predestination in Early Islam*. London: Luzac, 1948.

Weisberg, Richard Chadbourn. *The Politics of Crude Oil Pricing in the Middle East, 1970–1975: A Study in International Bargaining*. Berkeley: Institute of International Studies, University of California, 1977.

Williams, John Alden, ed. *Islam*. New York: Braziller, 1961.

Winder, R. Bayly. *Saudi Arabia in the Nineteenth Century*. New York: St. Martin's, 1965.

Al-Yassini, Ayman. *Religion and State in the Kingdom of Saudi Arabia*. Boulder, Colo.: Westview, 1985.

Yergin, Daniel. *The Prize: The Epic Quest for Oil, Money, and Power*. New York: Simon and Schuster, 1990.

Young, Arthur N. *Saudi Arabia: The Making of a Financial Giant*. New York: New York University Press, 1983.

al-Zaydi, Mshari. "King Abdullah's Vision for Saudi Arabia." *Al-Sharq al-Awsat*, February 21, 2009.

Index

David E. Long is a Middle East specialist concentrating on Saudi Arabian, Middle East, and Gulf affairs and on international terrorism. He is a retired diplomat, professor, and author of numerous books and articles on these areas of specialization.

Sebastian Maisel is assistant professor of Arabic and Middle East studies at Grand Valley State University, Allendale, Michigan. He has conducted anthropological fieldwork in Saudi Arabia and other Middle Eastern countries and has written books and articles on various topics related to Middle Eastern society, politics, and culture.